Women's History Tour
of the Twin Cities

WOMEN'S HISTORY TOUR
OF
THE TWIN CITIES

by

Karen Mason
and
Carol Lacey

Deborah Carlson,
editor and illustrator

Nodin Press
Minneapolis, Minnesota

ISBN 0-931714-17-6

Photo Credits: *St. Paul Dispatch-Pioneer Press* photo, Minnesota Historical Society, *Representatives Hannah Kempfer and Mabeth Hurd Paige,* page 13.

From a postcard published by The Acmegraph Company (Chicago), Minnesota Historical Society, *St. Joseph's Hospital,* page 19.

C. J. Hibbard and Company (Minneapolis) photo, Minnesota Historical Society, *Young Quinlan Store,* page 57.

Nodin Press, a Division of Micawber's Inc., 525 North Third Street, Minneapolis, MN 55401.

Printed by North Central Publishing Company.

This book is dedicated to Gretchen Kreuter

A founder of Women Historians of the Midwest, who has
inspired many women to discover their histories.

ACKNOWLEDGMENTS

The authors wish to thank:

Women Historians of the Midwest for conceiving the idea of and sponsoring the research for a women's history tour.

Members of the Women Historians of the Midwest steering committee for sharing their knowledge of and sources about women in the Twin Cities.

The Saint Paul Foundation and Minnesota Historical Society for financial support of the tour research.

Minnesota Historical Society for permission to use pictures. Bonnie Wilson and audio-visual library staff members of the Historical Society were very cooperative and helpful.

University of Minnesota Press for permission to use quotation from *Letters From the Promised Land: Swedes in America, 1840-1914.*

Marjorie Bingham, Sally Carlson, Sara Evans, Gretchen Kreuter and Kathy O'Brien for reading drafts of the tour and providing useful criticism.

Gretchen Kreuter for her contributions to the "Minnesota Pioneers," "Social Class, Social Service, Education" and "Domesticity and the Nuclear Family" portions of the tour.

Elizabeth Faue for information about Eva McDonald Valesh.

Annamarie Faue-Stemfly for information on the Strutwear strike.

Pat Murphy for comments about the architecture of some buildings included in the tour.

Rachel Mason for her help in shaping the research into a tour of the Twin Cities.

Laurie Stroope and Harriet Paske for information about the Young People's Symphony Association and Thursday Musical.

Students in Carol Lacey's "Women in Minnesota Life" class for their interest in exploring the history of local women.

The American Studies Association for the initial presentation of the tour at the organization's Seventh Biennial Convention in 1979.

Joan and Gene Mason for their advice and support.

Friends and colleagues for their suggestions and comments.

Deborah Carlson for her invaluable assistance in all stages of the project.

PREFACE:

The Nature of Women's History

Before commencing, a word on women's history and on the nature of this tour is in order. The women represented in this tour include factory workers and shop owners, servants and political activists, volunteers and career women, prominent individuals and nameless groups. Buildings or business enterprises serve as physical reminders of the accomplishments of some of these women; if we are not familiar with their work, we have at least heard their names. Most of the women, however, are anonymous; we can reconstruct the outlines of their lives as workers or home-makers but not the details. They are known to us only as figures in the census or as undifferentiated members of groups. All of these women, as well as the many whose experiences are not included in this tour, were makers of history. Their daily activities, whether in their homes or in the community, are what constitute history. It is the task of historians of women to reconstruct that history.

Traditionally, history has been concerned with politics and with formal arrange-ments of power. Historians wrote about wars, nation-building, and presidential elections. Recently there has been an effort to write history "from the bottom-up" —to include those people who were not part of the formal power structure. Histor-ians have looked at the effects of race, class, ethnicity, and religious affiliation as factors influencing the behavior of individuals and groups. They have examined voting patterns to learn about grass roots participation in politics and have studied demography to learn about the family and social change.

In addition to these traditional concerns, historians of women are interested in the role of gender in shaping women's lives. In other words, how did the fact of being female make the experience of women different from that of men? What would history be like if seen through the eyes of women? We must ask questions different from those traditionally addressed by historians in order to understand how women of various classes or races and of various times lived their lives.

Women's history is an attempt to write the history of all women, not just a privi-leged few. Thus, we must look at factors other than acclaim or success in the public sphere. We must examine women at work and in their homes, women in their rela-tions with others, women as community builders and as transmitters of culture.

Certain problems are inherent in the nature of a tour. We felt compelled to include the histories of some women for whom no commemorative structure or site remains. Just as preservation of historical documents has tended to favor the elite, so has preservation of historic buildings. A few of the sites provide an opportunity for returning in time to the periods discussed in the tour: the Alexander Ramsey house, for example, has been restored to its original state and is open to the public. As you view this building, imagine what it must have been like to be Anna Ramsey or, by contrast, what the daily routine of one of her servants would have been.

Some buildings are still standing, if in a somewhat changed form. The heavy exterior of the North Star Woolen Mill offers clues to the atmosphere in which young working women spent their days: one can envision large, dark rooms crowded with workers and noisy machinery.

In instances where no building remains, we have tried to include photographs. Where none are included, you are left to your own imagination to recreate what once existed, with assistance, perhaps, from nearby buildings that date from the period.

We have included diverse women in this tour. Certainly there are many noteworthy individuals who have been omitted. Had we been able to discuss all the "notable" women of the Twin Cities (an impossible task, no doubt), we would still have left out the countless women whose stories are unknown to us. But history is always a matter of choices, choosing which facts and people to emphasize, which to omit. Our aim in this tour has been to present a sampler of the experiences of Twin Cities women, not a comprehensive history. This is an invitation to the history of women in the Twin Cities.

INTRODUCTION:

Early History of the Twin Cities

A tour is by its nature ordered geographically rather than chronologically and can therefore be confusing to persons unfamiliar with the history of the area. This introduction is an attempt to provide a context for the tour: it gives a brief overview of the early settlement and growth of the Twin Cities as well as a summary of the major patterns of involvement of women in that development.

The first people known to have lived in the area that is now the Twin Cities were Sioux and Ojibway. The Kaposia band of Sioux resided near the junction of the Minnesota and Mississippi Rivers as early as 1700. The site of the village of Kaposia varied over the next century and a half but remained near the river junction. At the time St. Paul was being settled by whites in the 1840s and early 1850s the village of Kaposia was located at what is now South St. Paul.

The Sioux were a nomadic people and did not live in their villages all year round. In September the women, children and older men travelled north to gather rice while the young and middle-aged men went on the hunt. When the hunting season ended in late January, the families returned to the vicinity of their villages. Rather than living in the tepees or bark huts of their villages that were unprotected from winter storms, they lived in the woods nearby. During the summer months the Sioux planted crops such as corn and pumpkins. Soil preparation, planting, cultivation, and harvesting were all done by women.

In 1819 a fort was established at the junctions of the Minnesota and Mississippi Rivers. Called Fort St. Anthony in its early years, the name was changed to Fort Snelling in 1825. The first white women to reside in the Twin Cities area were wives of officers and soldiers at Fort Snelling. The officers' wives taught school and Sunday school to their children and started a Bible school for the adults at the Fort. They also assumed various housekeeping functions and organized social events to make the Fort seem more homelike. Besides the officers' wives, the only women living at the Fort were those needed for specific jobs, such as laundress.

In the 1830s there were about one thousand Indians living in the area that is now the Twin Cities. A number of women came to Minnesota from Eastern states in that decade to serve as missionaries to these Indians. Reverend Jedediah Stevens of the American Board of Commissioners for Foreign Missions, a Presbyterian-Congregational group, established a mission at Lake Harriet in 1835. With him came his wife, two sons, and adopted daughter Jane DeBow. Stevens started two schools. One was for Indian children and was taught by his niece, who learned to speak the Dakota language. The other was a small boarding school for mixed-blood daughters of traders and army officers. While Stevens himself had difficulty learning the Dakota language, Jane played with Sioux children and soon learned to speak Dakota; she was often called upon to interpret for her father. Jane DeBow later married Heman Gibbs and settled on a farm north of where the St. Paul Campus of the University of Minnesota is now located.

White settlers began to arrive in St. Paul in the early 1840s. When Harriet Bishop, a 30-year-old Baptist woman from Vermont, arrived in 1847 to teach school, she found a village consisting of a "few neat frame cottages . . . and a log cabin" and about 150 residents, excluding the Indian population. Most of these residents were French-Canadian or French-American; by Bishop's account only six of the families were "American" (presumably that meant native-born and English-speaking persons). In the next three years, however, St. Paul grew to a population of over 1000. By 1850, the year after Minnesota Territory was established, there were more than 350 families in St. Paul and about one third of the population was native-born. Two schoolhouses had been constructed and a Catholic church and four Protestant congregations established. By the 1860 census, the population of St. Paul had grown to 10,401.

In the late 1840s the village of St. Anthony grew up along the east side of the Mississippi River a few miles upstream from St. Paul, shortly before settlement began on the west side of the river in Minneapolis. Water power attracted settlers to St. Anthony; in the 1850s a large lumbering industry was developed and by the 1860s a flour milling center had begun to evolve. In the short span from 1848 to 1855 St. Anthony's population had swelled from 330 to nearly 3,000 residents. In the next fifteen years, however, it grew by only 2,000 residents. Minneapolis, by contrast, had expanded from a village of 3,391 persons in 1857 to a city of 13,066 by 1870. In 1872 Minneapolis and St. Anthony were united into a single city.

In this period of rapid expansion from the 1840s to the 1880s, immigrants arrived in Minnesota from Eastern states and from numerous foreign countries, chief among them Germany, Sweden, and Norway, but also Canada, Ireland, England, Czechoslovakia, Denmark, Russia, Poland—almost every European country.

Women performed vital functions both within and outside the home during these early years of settlement. They played a vital role in developing the churches and schools of the cities. In 1849 women in St. Paul formed a sewing society in order to raise funds with which to construct a schoolhouse. Early churches in the Twin Cities depended upon women's fundraising activities for financial support. The church fairs and suppers sponsored by women's organizations were also welcome social events.

From the earliest years of the Twin Cities' existence, women took the initiative to care for needy residents. In 1854, the Sisters of St. Joseph opened the state's first hospital, St. Joseph's Hospital in St. Paul. During the Civil War women formed "volunteer aid" societies to make, collect, and purchase supplies for the soldiers. By the 1870s women were involved in a wide variety of benevolent activities. They founded orphan asylums, homes for unwed mothers, and residences for homeless women. Through such organizations and institutions, women provided social services for which the state had not yet taken responsibility.

Women also worked—as unpaid volunteers or occasionally as paid employees—to establish some of the major cultural institutions of the Twin Cities. They collected funds and recruited artists and musicians for the Minneapolis Symphony, the Minneapolis Institute of Arts and the International Institute, only to have men take over the positions of power. Despite their contributions and commitment to these efforts, women saw their central position in educational and cultural institutions diminishing as the Twin Cities developed.

While some women had leisure time to devote to social service and cultural activities, many others had to work in order to support themselves or contribute to the family income. A few held professional positions such as physicians or lawyers. Many were teachers. But the majority were wage earners who worked in factories or shops or in domestic service. Many of them were young, single women living away from home or with their families. Some had emigrated from Europe, others from rural areas in the Midwest. Job opportunities may have been limited in the earliest years of St. Paul and Minneapolis, but by the 1880s there were many jobs open to women. The first Biennial Report of the Minnesota Bureau of Labor Statistics, for 1887-88, showed that women worked in factories, woolen mills, laundries, and restaurants; as clerks, stenographers, telegraph operators, dressmakers, and domestic servants; and in a variety of other occupations.

From the experiences of this wide variety of women this women's history tour has been fashioned. It concerns anonymous women and prominent women, what they achieved and how they lived their lives. This is not intended as a comprehensive history of women's involvement in the growth and development of the Twin Cities. Rather, it is a sample of what women's lives were like and of the impact these lives had in many dimensions of the Twin Cities' development.

MINNESOTA PIONEERS
TOUR

Representatives Hannah Kempfer and Mabeth Hurd Paige, 1941

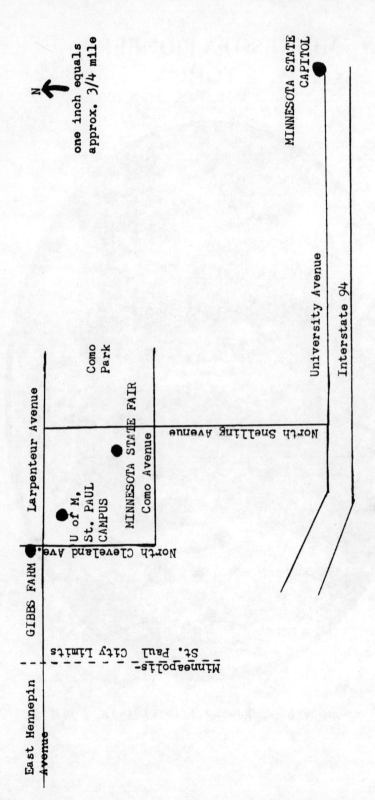

N

one inch equals
approx. 3/4 mile

MINNESOTA STATE
CAPITOL

University Avenue

Interstate 94

Larpenteur Avenue

Como
Park

MINNESOTA STATE FAIR

Como Avenue

North Snelling Avenue

U of M,
St. PAUL
CAMPUS

North Cleveland Ave.

GIBBS FARM

East Hennepin
Avenue

Minneapolis-
St. Paul City Limits

14

GIBBS FARM MUSEUM
Cleveland and Larpenteur Avenues
St. Paul, MN 55113

The Gibbs Farm Museum is restored in a manner characteristic of middle-class farmhouses of the 1860s and 1870s. The farmhouse's first occupants were Heman and Jane DeBow Stevens Gibbs. Jane had been "boarded out" by her parents when she was seven years old, because they could no longer care for her. Adopted by a missionary to the Indians, she grew up with Dakota and Lacota tribes and learned their language. She married Heman Gibbs in 1849, persuaded him not to go to California to seek gold, and with him took up a claim on this site, where they erected a shanty of logs and sod. The present structure, a comfortable two-story frame house, was built in 1867, and it is equipped today with some of the Gibbs family's original china and furnishings.

Owned by the Ramsey County Historical Society, the Gibbs Farm is open to the public from May through December. The original lady of the house, Jane Gibbs, was not a conventional nineteenth-century woman. She preferred hunting game and helping with field work to the weaving, spinning, candle-dipping and soap-making that occupied most pioneer women's lives. Nevertheless, one can see demonstrations of these womanly arts and crafts today at the Gibbs Farm, and one can learn more about Jane from the account of her life written by her daughter, Lillie, entitled *Little Bird that was Caught*.

Adjacent to the house is a one-room schoolhouse, restored and furnished as it was around the turn of the century. For many years a school was located near the Gibbs home, and often the schoolteacher, almost invariably female, lived with them. One room of the Gibbs house is furnished as it might have been when used by a teacher.

UNIVERSITY OF MINNESOTA
St. Paul Campus

South of the Gibbs Farm is the St. Paul Campus of the University of Minnesota where, in 1897, women were admitted to the Agricultural College and given "an opportunity to prepare themselves for their duties in farmers' homes." Many educators by then had come to believe that the traditional skills women had learned from their mothers and grandmothers could be more systematically and effectively taught. Male students on the St. Paul Campus commemorated the admission of women with a poem:

> Ah, what visions rise before us, of the halcyon days in store,
> Dreams of trousers neatly ironed, stockings out at heels no more,
> Butter fresh and sweet and golden, molded into cunning pats,
> Cheeses tied with bab ribbons, just the cutest little flats.
> Welcome sisters, to our classrooms: welcome later to our homes.
> It shall be our care that never one of you unmarried roams.

MINNESOTA STATE FAIR GROUNDS
St. Paul

The State Fair Grounds is east of the St. Paul Campus. Although the Minnesota State Fair now tries to provide all things to all people, it retains much of the character of earlier decades and evidences of the state's pioneer and rural heritage and values. The State Fair, where since 1885 women have brought the fruits of their labors in cookery and expressions of their creativity in domestic arts and crafts, is an appropriate location for a large statue commemorating the state's pioneer women and a building, a large log cabin, in honor of Territorial Pioneer Women. All women who lived in the Territory before it was admitted to the Union (May 11, 1858), and all female descendants of such women, can be members of the Territorial Pioneer Women's Club, which was established in 1899 to "bring the pioneer women of the state unto mutual acquaintance and social helpfulness" and "to perpetuate through their descendants the history and early settlement of Minnesota ..."

MINNESOTA STATE CAPITOL
St. Paul

Four miles southeast of the Fair Grounds is the State Capitol Building. At the Capitol one enters territory of a very different kind of woman pioneer: one who rocked the cradle, but who often also rocked the boat, even before voting or office-holding were legal.

It was Minnesota women's interest in social justice that caused concern about the limitations of disenfranchisement. Jane Grey Swisshelm, St. Cloud newspaper editor known for her attacks in the 1850s on the Democratic bosses of the Minnesota Territory, lectured here before the Senate in 1862 on the legal disabilities of women. In the rotunda there is a plaque in honor of another pioneer, Clara Ueland, identified with social reform and all programs in the interests of better conditions of living for women and children. Ueland was president of the Minnesota Woman Suffrage Association from 1914 until the vote was won five years later, and she organized the entire state on behalf of woman suffrage, raised large sums of money, and persuaded many prominent women to join the cause. On the day that the Nineteenth Amendment was finally ratified in Minnesota, the women who had filled the galleries during the final vote served a chicken dinner to the legislators, to demonstrate their gratitude. Clara Ueland went on to become the first president of the Minnesota League of Women Voters and then was active in lobbying for League-sponsored bills to protect women workers, ensure child welfare, and promote social hygiene. She died in 1927.

The other woman commemorated in the Capitol rotunda is Martha Ripley, physician and founder of Maternity Hospital in Minneapolis. She is remembered here because of her work on behalf of woman suffrage as well as for serving humanity "with farsighted vision and sympathy."

No plaques and no statues yet commemorate Anna Dickie Olesen, the first female candidate (in 1922) for the United States Senate endorsed by a major party, or the first four women who, in the same election year, won seats in the state House of Representatives. Of Mabeth Hurd Paige, Myrtle A. Cain, Sue M. Dickey Hough, and Hannah Kempfer, the *Minneapolis Tribune,* wrote: "Four feathered hats draw all eyes as Legislature convenes."

Women are no longer so rare in the legislative halls nor their hats so newsworthy. Although for several years Minnesota was the only state with feminist caucuses in both political parties, female members of the legislature are still only a small minority of the House and a smaller minority of the state Senate.

SOCIAL CLASS
SOCIAL SERVICE
EDUCATION
TOUR

St. Joseph's Hospital, about 1911

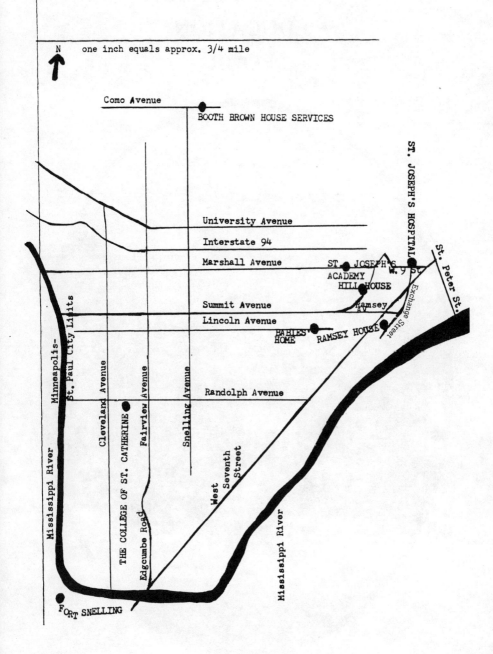

FORT SNELLING
St. Paul, MN 55111

Although America was a democratic republic by the time white settlement began in Minnesota, there were always significant social and economic differences among persons. These differences prevailed, of course, among women as well as men. In fact, women were often the means by which their husbands or fathers demonstrated their social status. The frontier sometimes exerted a "leveling" influence, but this was usually temporary and was so understood by everyone. Women on the frontier often revealed, in their letters and diaries, that they longed to live more like their sisters in the "civilized" East.

Class differences were clearly preserved at Fort Snelling. The Fort, built in 1818, was mostly a man's world. Soldiers could not be married when they enlisted, though some acquired wives later in their services. Officers could be married, but not many prospective wives cherished the thought of wintering at a primitive fort deep in Minnesota Territory.

As the years passed, and settlement proceeded, more women became a part of the life of the Fort. Officers' wives organized dances and musicales, decorated their homes as lavishly as money would permit, and generally attempted to recreate the life of genteel womanhood that a professional man's wife would be expected to lead. Female servants were a part of that life. Although their pay was low, some servants—those who were laundresses rather than employees in individual quarters—could earn more by working long hours for piece-work rates than enlisted men who were on fixed wages.

RAMSEY HOUSE
265 South Exchange Street
St. Paul, MN 55102

When Anna and Alexander Ramsey came to Minnesota from Pennsylvania in 1849, they lived for one year in a log house covered with board siding, a far cry from the grand stone house in which they would later reside. Anna Ramsey was not particularly enamored of Minnesota that first winter, though she later loved the area. St. Paul consisted of about 100 buildings, most of them built of rough logs, when Alexander Ramsey arrived to begin his service as first Territorial Governor of Minnesota. In late 1850 the Ramseys moved into a large frame house on the corner of Walnut and Exchange Streets at the edge of town. By the time this house was completed in 1872, Irvine Park had become one of the most fashionable neighborhoods in St. Paul.

Residence in the house on Exchange was a mixed blessing for Anna Ramsey. As the wife of one of Minnesota's leading citizens, she was expected to fulfill the role of hostess for many social and charitable events. And though she was later described as a "shining exemplar of true womanhood," it appears from her letters that she did not always cherish the role. "It is a perfect annoyance to be continually asked for the use of my parlor," she wrote to her daughter.

Like other women of the middle and upper classes in the nineteenth century, Anna Ramsey was involved in charitable organizations formed to aid the city's needy residents. She served for seven years as vice president of the board of managers of the Home for the Friendless, a St. Paul residence for homeless, destitute, and sick women that was established by the Ladies Christian Union in 1869. After Anna Ramsey's death in 1884 her daughter, Marion Ramsey Furness, served on the board of the Home.

The duties of managers included fundraising, deciding on admissions to the Home, and obtaining supplies for the Home. Each woman on the board served as visiting manager at the Home for one month about once a year. Visiting managers were required to go to the house twice a week to help oversee the operation of the Home, to resolve any problems that arose, to aid the matron in her work, and to report to the board at the monthly meeting on the affairs of the Home and the condition of the residents. The Home for the Friendless later limited its efforts to caring for the elderly and in 1935 was renamed the Protestant Home of St. Paul.

Anna Ramsey lived in the house on Exchange until her death. Thereafter, her daughter, Marion Furness, assumed the responsibilities of hostess; she continued to live in the house with her two daughters after her father's death in 1903. The house was willed to the Minnesota Historical Society by Marion Furness's daughters, Laura and Anna Furness, and became the Society's property in 1964. It is now open to the public for tours.

While Anna Ramsey and other well-to-do St. Paul and Minneapolis women enjoyed the luxury of fashionable houses, it was the work of domestic servants that made such a lifestyle possible. The servants, many of whom were young immigrant women, lived in cramped quarters on the third floors of these homes or in carriage houses situated behind the main houses. The third floor of the Ramsey house, for example, contained three bedrooms for servants as well as a nursery and an attic.

Many of the domestic servants were young Swedish girls who came to the Twin Cities in the last quarter of the nineteenth century and early part of the twentieth century. The waves of immigration at this time brought many Swedes to Minnesota. Those who came in family groups settled primarily in rural areas. By contrast, the vast majority of those who came to the Twin Cities were single, unskilled, and comparatively young. While the men found work in railroads, timber and flour mills, breweries, and construction companies, some of the women worked in the garment industries or as cleaning women in downtown Minneapolis offices. But most of the young Swedish women worked as domestics in the homes of upper class Americans. Families who lived in the Kenwood neighborhood of Minneapolis or along Summit Avenue in St. Paul often had Swedish girls working for them.

A young girl who emigrated to St. Paul from Sweden in the 1880s found work with an English family with three children. She described her work in a letter to her sister in Sweden in 1888:

"We are two girls. The first two months I was what we call at home a chambermaid, then I had to clean house and wait on the table the best I could. It was not so good you can be sure as long as I couldn't understand what they were talking about but then I had a Swedish girl as a comrade so she could interpret. She was kind to me and talked for me as good as she could. A little while before Christmas she left and then I had to take her place and I have had it since then.

"I am now glad because I believe the worst time is over. I can soon understand almost everything they say, for it is hardest the first half year as long as you can't manage the language, but if you only can happen to find decent folks to work for it goes well and good humor is something wherever you go.

"I must tell you now what my work is, it is to cook food, wash, and iron. I wash clothes every Monday and Tuesday, then I iron, and also Wednesday I have to iron sometimes, and bake on Thursdays and on Fridays I only have the cooking.

"I wonder if you have to iron anything? Now I will tell you that I have to iron as much as I want, I have two starched shirts to iron every week. At first I was so scared they would be ruined but now I shine them up so that they are like a mirror ... I wonder if you are thinking some about America now, you have never mentioned it. I think it would be so much fun if you came here. I don't think you would be homesick for I at least have not been homesick the slightest bit since I came here. I think that it is here like in Sweden, but better, because I would not earn more in Sweden than I get here ..."

> from Barton, H. Arnold. *Letters From the Promised Land: Swedes in America, 1840-1914.* University of Minnesota Press, Minneapolis. Copyright 1975 by the University of Minnesota.

BABIES' HOME
846 Lincoln Avenue
St. Paul, MN 55105

With the rapid pace of urbanization in the late nineteenth century came a rapid multiplication of social needs. Because most Americans believed that government had no obligation to meet these needs, private initiative—often female initiative—had to do the job instead. The Babies' Home of St. Paul is an example of the efforts of local women to meet a perceived social problem.

In January of 1890, a number of St. Paul women, many of whom lived in this neighborhood, met to discuss the possibility of caring for a "few of the frail little bodies born to misery and suffering in our city." There were several orphanages in the city at this time, but none of them accepted babies under the age of two.

The Babies' Home was incorporated with the purpose of caring for destitute, abandoned, and orphaned infants. A nurse was hired and in February, 1890, the Home began accepting babies in a small house on Summit Place. The Home was financed through annual subscriptions, cash contributions, fundraising parties, and fairs. Donations of food, clothing, and services were also accepted and a doctor offered his services to the Home free of charge.

The Home was soon filled and for a time the executive committee felt obliged to find places outside the Home for babies who could not be accommodated there. In 1891, however, the Babies' Home was moved to a larger house at 846 Lincoln.

In the first fifteen months of operation eighty-seven babies were cared for; by the end of four years the number had risen to 291. Some of these infants were later reclaimed by their parents or taken by friends, others were adopted, and a few died. At the physician's request, boarding places in the country were found for babies during the hot summer months. An attempt was also made to help the mothers of some of the babies by giving them employment in the Home or by helping them find employment elsewhere.

SUMMIT AVENUE
St. Paul, MN 55102 and 55105

Early St. Paul developed geographically in a way that perfectly exemplified class distinctions. In the lowlands along the banks on both sides of the Mississippi River, warrens of small homes of working-class and immigrant families developed throughout the second half of the nineteenth century. High on the bluffs above were the homes of the great and the affluent. Summit Avenue *was* the summit of St. Paul society. Not all its homes were as imposing as the residence of James J. Hill (240 Summit) and his family, but many were striking in their dimensions.

After decades of decline, Summit Avenue has been restored to much of its former elegance and it has been called the best-preserved Victorian boulevard in America. The grandchildren of immigrant servant girls now rent, at prices their grandmothers would have found inconceivable, the carriage houses and servants' quarters that have become fashionable in recent years.

Inside these Victorian homes, the ideals of True Womanhood were honored—sometimes in the breach, perhaps, but honored nonetheless. Few women could be ignorant of those ideals: purity, piety, domesticity, and submissiveness were extolled from a thousand pulpits, echoed in the women's magazines of the century, and taught by mother to daughter. Women were supposed to be a civilizing influence upon their menfolk, and they could be so only by adhering as nearly as possible to the demands of the cult of True Womanhood.

These were middle-class ideals, but many of the servant girls of Summit Avenue aspired to the economic security and social status that was necessary to achieve them.

ST. JOSEPH'S ACADEMY
355 Marshall Avenue
St. Paul, MN 55102

ST. JOSEPH'S HOSPITAL
69 West Exchange Street
St. Paul, MN 55102

According to the canons of proper female behavior, women were not supposed to lead, organize, administer, or otherwise exercise power. If they did, they would lose their femininity. So, at least, it was thought in the nineteenth century, when the city of St. Paul experienced its greatest growth.

However, there was another much older tradition that permitted women to organize and administer without incurring social disapproval: the tradition of Catholic women. In new towns and cities, nuns often took the lead in founding social welfare and educational institutions. The Sisters of St. Joseph performed this function in Minnesota.

In 1851, four Sisters of St Joseph, recently arrived by steamer from Carondelet, near St. Louis, Missouri, founded St. Joseph's Academy, a school for girls. When it opened in the vestry of a log chapel in what is now downtown St. Paul, fourteen girls were in attendance. By the next year, enrollment had increased to such an extent that classes had to be conducted in the chapel itself. A two-story brick building was erected in 1852 and used until 1859, when the students were transferred to St. Joseph's Hospital for classes.

In 1863 the southwest section of this building on Marshall Avenue was completed; a chapel, classrooms, a parlor, music rooms, and library were located on the lower floors, while the third floor housed dormitory rooms. Because the Academy was located far from residential districts, it was mainly a boarding school until transportation facilities improved in the 1870s. St. Joseph's Academy closed in 1971.

The Sisters of St. Joseph also founded the first hospital in Minnesota. In the early 1850s, the small frame shanty in which the Sisters had at first resided was used as a temporary home for sick immigrants and the log chapel was converted into an infirmary for cholera patients. A four-story stone structure surrounded by walks and gardens was completed in 1854 at Ninth and Exchange. Besides functioning as a hospital, this building housed an orphanage and the novitiate. City and county patients as well as private patients were admitted to the hospital; if they could not pay the charge of eight dollars a week, they were treated at no cost. St. Joseph's Hospital is still in operation on the same site as the first stone structure.

THE COLLEGE OF ST. CATHERINE
2004 Randolph Avenue
St. Paul, MN 55105

A women's college founded in 1905 by the Sisters of St. Joseph of Carondelet, St. Catherine's was in some ways a daring experiment. Although higher education for women was not new by 1905, the ideas of Mother Antonia McHugh, its early dean and president, were. She believed that the sisters on her faculty ought to have the best graduate education possible, and she sent them to secular universities in America and abroad to obtain their doctoral degrees. She believed that students ought not receive only training in the "womanly arts," but should receive a solid liberal arts education as well.

St. Catherine's was the first Catholic college to become accredited. When accrediting officials expressed concern over the college's small financial endowment, Mother Antonia pointed to St. Catherine's "living endowment"—the Sisters of St. Joseph, whose contributed services insured both the quality and continuity of the college. In 1937, The College of St. Catherine became the first Catholic college to be granted a chapter of Phi Beta Kappa.

BOOTH BROWN HOUSE SERVICES
1471 Como Avenue
St. Paul, MN 55108

As the United States underwent rapid urbanization and industrialization in the latter part of the nineteenth century, many young women migrated alone to cities from rural areas and foreign countries to find work. Living away from their families, young women were more vulnerable to seduction and abandonment. Thus, a rise in illegitimacy accompanied urbanization. Women's organizations established "rescue homes" in the Twin Cities in the 1870s and succeeding decades to cope with the problem; they often attempted to "reform" these "fallen" women as well as provide care and shelter during pregnancy.

In 1898 the Salvation Army founded the Women's Home and Hospital to serve as a home for unwed mothers, deserted women, and homeless women. At its first location in the Robbins residence at Jackson Street and University Avenue in St. Paul, eighteen adults and six children could be accommodated. Babies slept in padded orange crates, and second-hand hospital beds served as delivery tables. Drs. Jeanette McLaren and Katherine Nye provided the first medical services.

This house was soon filled to overflowing, so the agency moved to a slightly larger house in 1909. But within a few years the Hospital also outgrew this house, so a large brick Tudor-style building was constructed at 1471 Como Avenue. The new facility, which could accommodate fifty mothers and thirty-five babies, was opened in 1913 under the name Rescue Home: Maternity Home. In 1942 the name was changed to Booth Memorial Hospital.

In the late 1950s the St. Paul Public Schools sent a teacher to Booth to instruct school-age girls living at the home. This education program was expanded in the 1960s to include pregnant teenagers living elsewhere in the community. Many of the girls seeking care at Booth came from outlying counties; they often received their first prenatal care at Booth because they had been unwilling to reveal pregnancy to local doctors. In 1960 over 500 young women, most of them referred by social agencies, sought care at Booth.

As illegitimacy became less of a stigma in recent years and more unwed mothers began to keep their babies, the need for such a home declined. Although the Booth home for unwed mothers continued until 1974, the hospital closed in 1971. Booth Brown House Services is now a residential treatment center for emotionally disturbed adolescent girls.

ETHNICITY and
SOCIAL SERVICE
TOUR

Ladies Aid Society, Pilgrim Baptist Church, about 1900

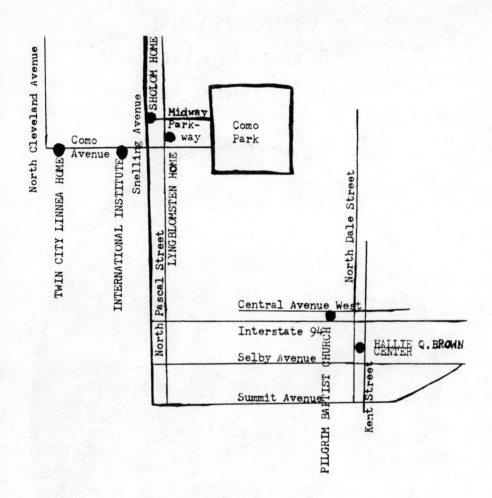

N

one inch equals approx. 3/4 mile

PILGRIM BAPTIST CHURCH
732 Central Avenue West
St. Paul, MN 55104

Blacks first came to Minnesota in the 1820s as servants of army officers at Fort Snelling. Major Lawrence Taliaferro, who was Indian agent at the Fort in the 1820s and 1830s, brought a number of slaves to Minnesota and later freed them. When Dred Scott came to Minnesota with army surgeon John Emerson in 1836, he married one of Taliaferro's slaves, Harriet Robinson.

Some of the blacks who were given their freedom settled in the hamlets outside the Fort in the 1830s, along with fur traders, discharged soldiers, and refugees from a Red River settlement. The 1850 census listed thirty-nine free black citizens in Minnesota Territory; by 1860 there were 259 black residents, whose occupations included tailor, postal employee, janitor, businessman, carpenter, and restaurant and hotel employee.

During the 1860s a number of blacks arrived in Minnesota. In 1863 a group of about 200 recently-freed slaves came up the Mississippi River by flatboat from Missouri, led by Robert T. Hickman, a black preacher. The group was refused landing at the St. Paul levee by hostile Irish dockworkers and so was forced to unload at Fort Snelling and walk back to St. Paul. Some of these blacks went to Minneapolis and Stillwater; those who remained in St. Paul became the nucleus of the city's black community and founded Pilgrim Baptist Church. Early meetings of the congregation were held in a music hall and in various other buildings in downtown St. Paul. Eventually, a church building was constructed on Sibley Street. The building now in use was constructed in 1928.

In the early years of the Church's existence when money was scarce and the pastor was paid largely in kind, the women of the Church formed a pastor's aid society in order to provide food, clothing, and other necessities for the pastor and his family. This organization was later called the Ladies Aid Society. Its members raised money for the Church and supported a variety of mission and benevolent causes, particularly aiding persons in the vicinity who were in need. Women were also active in the Church's social and literary society in the 1880s.

Because they were excluded from the recreation centers and organizations open to other St. Paul residents, many of the activities of black citizens centered around their churches and lodges. Welfare and educational services were concerns of these churches, while their fairs, parties, and carnivals were major sources of recreation for blacks. Pilgrim Baptist Church served as a meeting place for a variety of clubs. The Adelphai, for example, one of the oldest black women's organizations in Minnesota, held its fiftieth anniversary celebration at the Church. The Adelphai was founded in 1899 to do philanthropic work and to promote literacy among its members. A scholarship fund was established in 1936 to aid worthy students.

HALLIE Q. BROWN COMMUNITY CENTER
270 Kent Street
St. Paul, MN 55102

While various organizations and agencies such as the YMCA provided recreational facilities and meeting places for the white residents of St. Paul in the late nineteenth and early twentieth centuries, no such facilities existed for blacks. The YMCA, for example, had by 1923 admitted only four black men as members, all of them prominent citizens. The YWCA, on the other hand, had made several efforts to establish a "colored branch" but had dropped the program because of lack of interest and funds. Thus, churches and lodges served as the major centers of social activity for blacks.

In 1923, the St. Paul Urban League was formed by a group of black citizens. One of the League's first projects was the establishment of the Hallie Q. Brown Community Center as a recreation and meeting place. At the time of its founding in 1929, the Center was housed in a small frame building at 598 West Central Avenue. The next year it was moved to the old Union Hall built by the black lodges of St. Paul at 553 Aurora Avenue. Since 1972, when the Martin Luther King Center opened, Hallie Q. Brown and several other social agencies have been located there.

The Center was named for Hallie Quinn Brown (ca. 1850-1949), a black teacher, writer, and advocate of temperance and women's rights. A native of Ohio, Brown lectured throughout the nation and in Europe. She visited the Center in 1929 and again in 1947.

The Center's first two directors were black women; I. Myrtle Carden served as director from the time the Center opened in 1929 until 1949. She had previously been director of the Sharpe Street Settlement House in Baltimore. Carden was succeeded by Alice Sims Onque, a native of St. Paul who had worked in New York community centers.

I. Myrtle Carden hoped that the programs at the Hallie Q. Brown Center would counteract the influences of the pool halls, taverns, game casinos, cabarets, and dance halls located in the neighborhood in the 1930s. She helped develop a program focused upon the family that included home nursing and hygiene courses and well-baby and dental clinics in addition to music, craft, and athletic programs for children. There were also programs for adults and senior citizens. During the Depression a free nursery school was established; it served as an all-day child care center for children of working mothers during World War II.

Because it was hoped that the Center would improve relations between blacks and whites, all residents of the Summit-University neighborhood were welcomed when the Center opened in 1929. It has become a multi-cultural center, although it is administered and supported mainly by blacks.

TWIN CITY LINNEA HOME
2040 Como Avenue
St. Paul, MN 55108

LYNGBLOMSTEN HOME
1298 North Pascal Street
St. Paul, MN 55108

The Linnea Society is an example of a benevolent organization formed by a particular ethnic group to aid others of the same nationality. In 1904 a group of Swedish women from Minneapolis established the Linnea Society as a home for Swedish female servants and elderly women who had no homes or relatives. A similar society was organized in St. Paul a few months later.

Anna Bennett, who initiated the founding of the St. Paul group, had made an unsuccessful earlier attempt to organize benevolent work; at the suggestion of a midwife that she put her talents to work "doing good," Mrs. Bennett had invited several prominent St. Paul women to a coffee party to discuss her proposition. But not one of them came to the party. When she took up the cause again, Anna Bennett invited Swedish homemakers like herself to meet with the founder of the Minneapolis Linnea Society. This time her efforts met with success.

Several of the women who helped found these societies had been domestics themselves and they knew that young immigrant servants were often "compelled to board at lodging houses, sometimes surrounded by unwholesome conditions and associates." They wished to open a home where domestics could stay while looking for employment.

The St. Paul and Minneapolis Linnea Societies joined in 1909 and incorporated as the Twin City Linnea Society. Society members spent several years raising funds and began building the Twin City Linnea Home at a location midway between the cities in October, 1917. The Society voted to admit aged men as well as women and when the Home opened in February, 1918, the first resident was a man; by October, all the rooms were filled. When it opened in 1918, the primary focus of the Linnea Home was elderly Swedes in need of a place to live, rather than young working women.

Swedish women were also responsible for founding the Bethesda Lutheran Home for Invalids in St. Paul in 1914 and the Scandinavian Union Relief Home in Minneapolis in 1915.

The Lyngblomsten Home for aged Norwegians was started by Minneapolis and St. Paul Norwegian women who met to form a literary society in 1902. Deciding that benevolent activity would be more satisfying, some of the women organized the Lyngblomsten Society. One of the major functions of the Society, like that of earlier charitable organizations formed by women, was fundraising, and the methods employed were similar to those of other women's benevolent societies. The Society held raffles, socials, quilting parties, waffle luncheons, and lutefisk suppers to raise funds for the Lyngblomsten Home, which opened in St. Paul in 1912. The Lyngblomsten Home Society grew so large that it had to split into circles, and branches were formed in a number of cities in Minnesota, Wisconsin and North Dakota.

SHOLOM HOME
1554 Midway Parkway (at Snelling Avenue)
St. Paul, MN 55108

Women played an important role in the development of the Jewish communities of St. Paul and Minneapolis. Like women of other religious and ethnic groups, they founded benevolent societies to aid the needy and organizations to provide financial aid and other forms of assistance to their congregations. The women of Mount Zion Hebrew Congregation in St. Paul, for example, founded the Ladies Hebrew Benevolent Society in 1871. In its first year of existence the Society secured a melodeon for the synagogue. In subsequent years the women held strawberry festivals to raise money for the cemetery fund. A Gentlemen's Relief Society was organized in the 1880s, but in 1895 its treasury was transferred to the Ladies Hebrew Benevolent Society; thenceforth the women did the actual relief work while the men served as an advisory body.

In addition to general relief work, women were responsible for founding such social service institutions as settlement houses and homes for the elderly. The Jewish Home for the Aged owed its origins to the Charity Loan Society, a women's organization founded in 1890 to provide loans to needy families. The group reorganized in 1903 as the Charity Loan Society and Old Women's Home and began to formulate plans for a home for the aged. The Society purchased a mansion at 75 Wilkin Street and in 1908 the home opened. A similar home was established in Minneapolis the same year, also through the efforts of a women's society. The Minneapolis and St. Paul Jewish communities decided to cooperate in their work and in 1923 a new building called the Jewish Home for the Aged of the Northwest was opened at Midway Parkway and Snelling Avenue in St. Paul to serve both cities. The Home merged with the George Kaplan Residence in 1971 to become the Sholom Home; in 1979 a new building was completed at the Midway location to house the Sholom Home, a non-profit Jewish nursing home.

INTERNATIONAL INSTITUTE
1694 Como Avenue
St. Paul, MN 55108

The International Institute, originally housed in a converted saloon on Rice Street, was one of a number of services created to help young women adjust to life in a new city. The Institute was founded in 1911 on the impetus of the national YWCA to serve young, foreign-born women by teaching them English and giving them legal aid when they applied for citizenship or endeavored to bring other family members to the United States. Another Institute objective was to help promote understanding among people of various cultures. Still celebrated today, the Festival of Nations was first held in 1932 under the direction of its founder Helen Sickels. The Festival gives Twin Citians a chance to sample the foods, crafts, music, and dancing of numerous ethnic groups.

The Institute's work in teaching English expanded also in 1932 when the Minnesota Department of Education discontinued all its free classes in English and citizenship. Language classes for foreign-born and refugees continue today at the Institute.

DOWNTOWN ST. PAUL
WALKING TOUR

Woman Suffrage Rally, Rice Park, St. Paul, 1914
(South of Landmark Center)

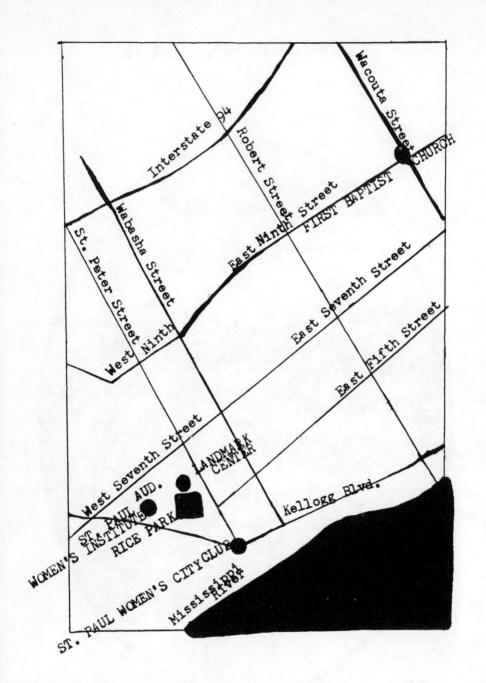

N

one inch equals approx. 1/8 mile

FIRST BAPTIST CHURCH
Wacouta and East Ninth Streets
St. Paul, MN 55101

In 1847, Harriet Bishop came to Minnesota to start a school. She had attended Catherine Beecher's teacher-training course back East where she had been told that women might fulfill their mission to nurture and educate the young by becoming schoolteachers. Filled with high resolve, Bishop arrived in St. Paul and within one week opened her first school in a log shack that had once been a blacksmith's shop. During the next two weeks she had established the town's first Sunday school which led to the founding of the First Baptist Church of St. Paul. Bishop was, in fact, the first Baptist in St. Paul, and for a while the only one. Her role in establishing the congregation is commemorated in a bas-relief on the door of the present church.

In 1848, Bishop helped found the St. Paul Circle of Industry, an organization of eight women that raised money to build a schoolhouse by selling sewn articles and by soliciting contributions from townspeople; the Industry members were proud that "the first payment on the lumber for the first schoolhouse was made with money earned with the needle by the ladies of this Circle."

Other social issues also occupied Bishop's attention—temperance, suffrage, and "moral reform" among them. In 1879, for example, the St. Paul Woman's Christian Temperance Union employed Bishop as a state organizer. Harriet Bishop was convinced that women had a special role as civilizers and reformers and once declared, with high hopes, "To woman is entrusted the future destiny of Minnesota."

LANDMARK CENTER/SCHUBERT CLUB   Rice Park/Suffrage Rally
75 West Fifth Street
St. Paul, MN 55102

Landmark Center, a grand old building saved only recently from the wrecker's ball, is the home of the Schubert Club, a musical organization that is a monument to generations of women who, like Harriet Bishop, took very seriously their "civilizing" mission to educate and to spread enthusiasm for "culture."

The Club was organized in 1882 by a group of St. Paul women and was called the Ladies' Musicale. In 1888 the name was changed to the Schubert Club. By then it had formally organized afternoon concerts and study groups, fortnightly recitals presented by Club members, and lectures and discussions by speakers with national reputations.

In 1892, the Club imported its first prominent musician: George Holmes, a bass who soloed frequently with Theodore Thomas's Chicago Orchestra. In the same year, directors of the Club announced that musical abilities of all active or performing members of the Schubert Club would be examined annually by a committee of accomplished artists. Those who failed the tests would be reduced to the rank of associate member. Quality was then, and continues to be, a central concern of the organization.

Other cultural and educational organizations have their offices in Landmark Center, and nearly all were founded by women—women of leisure a century ago, who demonstrated through their association with art and culture that they did not "need" to be employed in "productive" activity, but who also cared deeply about the progress of the arts in a new and rough-hewn community.

Across the street from Landmark Center is Rice Park where, in 1914, hundreds of men and women who cared about the progress of political equality, held a suffrage rally, almost seventy years after Harriet Bishop first spoke of suffrage in St. Paul and six years before the final passage of the Nineteenth Amendment.

ST. PAUL WOMEN'S INSTITUTE
St. Paul Auditorium, off Washington Street and Kellogg Boulevard
St. Paul, MN 55102

Gloomy war news came from Europe, the austerity of the Great Depression still lingered in St. Paul, yet 12,000 women turned out at the St. Paul Auditorium for the first Women's Institute program in 1939.

The Women's Institute was the brain-child of Ben and Agnes Kennedy Ridder, publishers of the *St. Paul Pioneer Press.* Two years earlier, Ben Ridder had begun a drive to bring prosperity to downtown St. Paul retailers. Surveying retail trade, he found $11 to $15 million going "over the bridge" to Minneapolis each year. He called in a dozen leaders of St. Paul women's organizations for help. Among these women was Agnes Kennedy, who responded, "Give us good reasons for spending our money here." Subsequently, she became director of the new Institute, and Ben's wife.

The Women's Institute was a series of monthly programs and performances, many of which were by nationally-recognized entertainers and lecturers. There was no secret that from the beginning the Institute was not a money-making proposition. Heavily underwritten by the newspaper (twenty-five to fifty thousand dollars a year), the monthly Institute programs did offer the needed incentive for women to come downtown to shop. And as an additional shopping-Institute link, retail merchants cooperated with special window displays related to the performance or program of the month.

Although the Institute directors were drawn conspicuously from the upper echelons of St. Paul society, patrons were mostly middle-class homemakers, club women, teachers or office workers. So eager were some of them for the best seats in the Auditorium that they would sleep out on the street the night before in order to be first in line for the bargain-priced tickets. For $2.40 a season (20 cents a performance), they had a chance to attend programs featuring Isaac Stern, Roger Williams, Eleanor Roosevelt, Gracie Fields, and a roster of Metropolitan Opera stars, to name a few. Also on the schedule were fashion shows, slides of Ridder trips to Europe and practical programs such as that given by S. Robert Anshen, West Coast architect, on "Your House and You," an analysis of home building costs and considerations.

The Institute turned out to be a smashing business success. St. Paul, and the Institute, attracted national media attention as women helped propel St. Paul from eleventh to fourth place among American cities in annual volume of retail sales per capita.

The Institute also branched out toward civic projects. In 1942, for example, Women's Institute members carried 30,000 pounds of scrap metal to the Auditorium for the war effort. In 1946, a city beautification drive, championed by the Institute with the slogan, "Every Lot a Beauty Spot," helped to trigger several hundred million dollars of expenditure in St. Paul for building construction and general city improvement.

As the St. Paul business community once more thrived, the Women's Institute, like the St. Paul Women's City Club, was dissolved in 1971.

ST. PAUL WOMEN'S CITY CLUB
St. Peter Street and Kellogg (originally Third) Boulevard
St. Paul, MN 55102

This four-story structure of smooth yellow stone with polished black granite trim, built in 1931 on the site where Harriet Bishop's first school was located, is one of the finest examples of art deco in the Twin Cities. The building was designed by Magnus Jemne, a Norwegian emigrant; Elsa Jemne designed the terrazo mosaic floor.

The Women's City Club was founded and incorporated with over 1000 members ten years earlier, in 1921, to meet a need that had become increasingly insistent by the time of the First World War. More and more women were playing active roles outside of their homes, whether as patrons of the arts, as clerks and secretaries, or as volunteer workers in various kinds of social and patriotic agencies. Men had clubs where they could meet and eat. Women needed the same. Membership in the Women's City Club was open to any woman who was interested in the goals of the Club and could pay the $10 annual membership fee.

The Women's City Club had been headquartered in three other downtown locations (first the old Minnesota Club at Fourth and Cedar, then 345 Minnesota Street, and, briefly, the new Minnesota Club on Washington Street) before eagerness for a building of their own led members to plan a series of fundraisers, several involving touring opera companies. Alice O'Brien, St. Paul philanthropist, world traveller and art connoisseur, who threw free tickets to one fundraiser opera while flying over St. Paul in a plane, was in charge of the building committee which, even during the Depression, produced the funds for this structure and paid remaining debts by 1937.

From the Club's beginning, it made rooms available to local organizations, and by the late 1930s the Club had become a center for many women's meetings. Among the groups that used its facilities were service organizations such as St. Paul Business and Professional Women, Zonta, Quota, Inter-Club Council, Gyro, and Thursday Club. Because of the Club's existence, many women kept in touch with each other and with the social, cultural, and political world. T.S. Eliot, Gertrude Stein, and a former St. Paul Central High School student, Amelia Earhart, lectured at the Women's City Club in the early 1930s, and local speakers in politics, government, international relations, and the arts were featured at membership meetings.

During World War II, Women's Recruitment Services requested the Club to sponsor teas to help recruit volunteers for United States Women's Service Organizations. The teas were not successful and recruiters had monthly quotas to meet, so the Club's Board of Directors decided to stage a mass recruitment rally in the St. Paul Auditorium. On October 1, 1943, "Miss America Marches" was scheduled for the

Auditorium. Local and national talent was arranged for this rally, and for the first time in history, the top officers of the six women's service organizations (Women's Army Corps, Army and Navy Nurse Corps, WAVES, U.S. Marine Women's Corps, and SPAR, the Coast Guard women's branch) appeared together with the result that enlistment quotas for the months ahead were met.

The Club's membership peaked in the 1950s and then began to decline. By the 1960s, there were many organizations and clubs that served women's needs, and younger women preferred less structured educational and social environments than what the Women's City Club offered. The building was, therefore, sold to the Minnesota Museum of Art in 1971.

UNIVERSITY WOMEN
TOUR

Maria L. Sanford

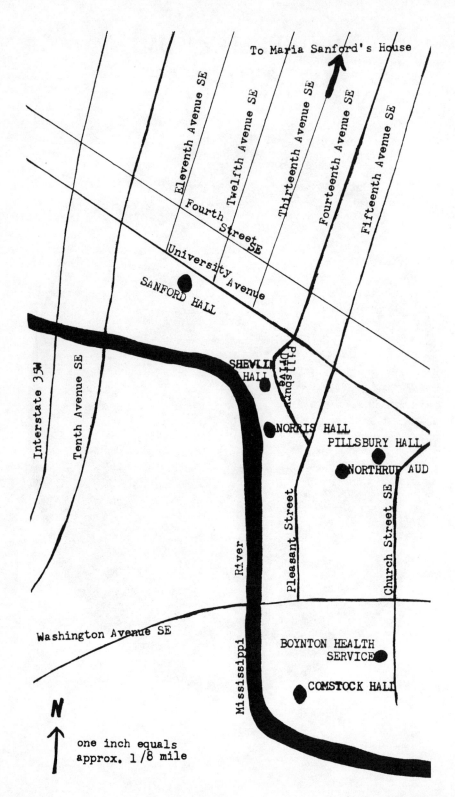

To Maria Sanford's House

Eleventh Avenue SE

Twelfth Avenue SE

Thirteenth Avenue SE

Fourteenth Avenue SE

Fifteenth Avenue SE

Fourth Street SE

University Avenue

SANFORD HALL

Interstate 35W

Tenth Avenue SE

SHEVLIN HALL

Pillsbury Drive

NORRIS HALL

PILLSBURY HALL

NORTHRUP AUD

Pleasant Street

Church Street SE

River

Mississippi

Washington Avenue SE

BOYNTON HEALTH SERVICE

COMSTOCK HALL

N

one inch equals
approx. 1/8 mile

SANFORD HALL
1100 University Avenue SE
Minneapolis, MN 55455

Maria Louise Sanford, teacher and lecturer, was born in Connecticut in 1836 to parents who taught their children the values of frugality, hard work, and education. Maria's mother supervised her precocious daughter's informal education with studies and memorization of poetry, stories of heroic Revolutionary War men and women, and large portions of the Bible. Maria used her dowry money to attend the New Britain Normal School. She graduated with honors at age nineteen and began teaching school (at $10 per month) forty miles from home. Although Maria Sanford had no more formal education, she continued to devour readings in history, sciences, and logic throughout her life.

In 1869 Swarthmore College in Pennsylvania invited her to take a temporary appointment as instructor of history and literature. The following year, she was made professor of public speaking and history—one of the first women professors in the United States. By this time her enthusiasm, her wish to create interest in the subject as a substitute for harsh student discipline, and her doubled attention to "unruly" or "slow" students, had been noted.

William Watts Folwell, first president of the University of Minnesota, met Maria Sanford in 1880 while he was on an eastern tour to find faculty members for the growing young "western" institution. After a half hour's conversation, he hired her as assistant professor of English at a salary of $1,200. Folwell later said: "The greatest thing I ever did for the University was to bring Maria Sanford here."

When Sanford came to the University, it was housed in one building, Old Main. It had a faculty of 18 and a student body of 300. Sanford was an unusual teacher, and her classes in composition, rhetoric, elocution and oratory soon were overflowing. She used lantern slides to illustrate her lectures. Thus, students, even though they were in rhetoric classes, became acquainted with art and architecture of Europe and the ancient world. During her second year at the University, Sanford became a full professor; in her third year, she served as acting head of the English Department. By the time of her retirement at age 72, Maria Sanford had taught 54 years, 29 of them at the University of Minnesota, where her Department of Rhetoric and Elocution was the University's largest.

Sanford's concern for students went beyond the classroom. She was known to coach orators at four a.m., and sixteen students lived in her house near the campus. Because living at Maria Sanford's house was popular among students, she bought a second house to accommodate roomers.

Surpassing her own reputation as an inspiring and imaginative teacher, Sanford became an accomplished religious preacher and lecturer sought after across the nation. After her retirement, she travelled a lecture circuit that went from Califor-

---

Note:

The first printed announcement of the establishment of the University of Minnesota appeared in 1868; three faculty members were listed. Helen Sutherland, the first woman teacher at the University, began in the 1871-72 academic year as assistant professor of Latin.

nia to Montana and east to New York. Her lectures covered a wide repertoire of subjects: poetry, social issues, art, politics. While she was still at the University, Sanford lectured in Minnesota four or five nights a week, even in winter, travelling from 50 to 100 miles a night. Yet she never missed a class. She was known throughout the state because of her popular lecture series for farmers, organized by the University, which helped to save the land-grant institution at a time when the legislature threatened to separate the academic and agricultural colleges.

Maria Sanford was also active in civic affairs. She was Director of Charitable Work at Northwestern Hospital. In 1903 she was appointed as Minnesota's delegate to the National Prison Association Congress. In 1914 she represented Minnesota at the Tenth Annual Conference of the National Child Labor Committee and the National Conference on Unemployment. As founder, in 1892, of the Minneapolis Improvement League, she organized projects to improve garbage and snow removal, prohibit spitting in streetcars, and stimulate planting of flowers. She encouraged public school children to participate in a city-wide competition for prize flowers, a project that won national attention.

The highlight of her academic career came in June, 1909, her last year as a faculty member, when she was asked to deliver the commencement address at the University. Maria Sanford was honored because this was the first time a woman had been asked to speak at a major university graduation. Here are some of her words:

> It is not some special genius conferred upon the few, but the wise use of the gifts common to all, that makes life rich and valuable . . . The moral of this for the University is plain. It may, it can, it should give to the youth of this State this awakening impulse; breathe into them this breath of life; rouse them not to mere physical courage, but to the courage of high convictions; give to them aims, ambitions, purposes, which shall transform, transfigure their whole lives.

Legend is that those who heard an oration by Maria Sanford never forgot her impressive style and power. But other tangible memorials to Sanford also exist. In 1910, her name was given to the first women's dormitory at the University of Minnesota, Sanford Hall. In 1916, on her eightieth birthday, the University held a statewide convocation of all its colleges in her honor, and a Minneapolis public school was named for her. A thirteen-year campaign by the Minnesota Federation of Women's Clubs prompted the placement of her statue as one of Minnesota's two representatives in the Hall of Statuary near the doors leading to the Senate Chamber in the National Capitol in Washington, D.C., during Minnesota's Centennial in 1958. Maria Sanford, "the best known and best loved woman in Minnesota," thus became the second woman to be so honored.

A modest frame house, near the campus at 1050 Thirteenth Avenue Southeast, was Sanford's home from 1905 until her death in 1920.

NORRIS HALL
172 Pillsbury Drive SE,
University of Minnesota
Minneapolis, MN 55455

When Dr. J. Anna Norris became director of the University's Department of Physical Education for Women in 1912, women's gym classes were held in one end of the Armory, the department office was in the balcony, and dressing rooms (two showers and a little tub) were in the basement. In those days, some women students cut gym class because they feared the crowds of cadets they had to pass to get to class in the Armory. Hygiene, Swedish gymnastics, dancing and a few outdoor sports were offered; all female students were required to take gym their first two years at the University, but because of inadequate facilities "the healthiest women were excused from classes."

Anna Norris had overcome odds before. A graduate of Boston Normal School of Gymnastics, she had applied to Harvard and Tufts medical schools, but was rejected because she was a woman. She then began systematically applying to all medical centers west of the Hudson River and finally was accepted by Northwestern University's medical school. She was graduated in 1900 and scored the highest of all taking the Cook County medical exams that year. Although she had earned her medical degree, she was not particularly interested in practicing medicine and directed her professional energy toward physical education.

At the end of her first year at Minnesota (where she came after holding several positions elsewhere in the nation), President George E. Vincent got legislative approval for a women's gymnasium; in 1914 the women moved into a gym of their own and the department grew rapidly. Emphasis shifted over the years from team sports to individual sports. The first teachers' training program started in 1919, and the first professionals graduated with physical education majors in 1922. Norris also contributed her services to the then-small University Health Service and helped to establish the practice of physical exams for each student. However, it was not just the growth and expansion of the physical education program, but its broad foundation of health, physical education and recreation that made it progressive for its time.

In her leadership, Dr. Norris was respected for her application of high medical and teaching standards, which in turn helped to establish the academic fields of health and physical education more solidly.

Upon Anna Norris's death in 1958, the Women's Gymnasium was renamed Norris Hall in her honor.

PILLSBURY HALL
310 Pillsbury Drive SE,
University of Minnesota
Minneapolis, MN 55455

Josephine Tilden, the first woman scientist hired by the University of Minnesota, began work as a graduate student and teaching assistant on the campus after receiving her bachelor's degree there in 1895. In 1897 she boldly announced her interest in studying algae of the Pacific Ocean, drawing much attention because she was a woman and because very little work had been done on algae in the Pacific.

Professor Tilden subsequently completed 13 field trips to the Pacific. The largest undertaking, conducted in 1935, two years before her retirement as professor of botany, involved a year-long expedition with ten graduate students, four of them women, collecting and studying more than 7,500 seaweed specimens along the shores of New Zealand, Tasmania and Australia. Among the results of this work was Josephine Tilden's prediction that seaweed would be next in order as human beings extended their search for food.

Tilden was considered a leading authority on algae and wrote more than 50 botanical publications, including *Minnesota Algae* (1910).

BOYNTON HEALTH SERVICE
410 Church Street SE,
University of Minnesota
Minneapolis, MN 55455

Just out of medical school in 1921, Ruth Boynton joined the University of Minnesota Health Service as a public health physician. In 1936, she was named head of the Health Service and Professor of Public Health. Dr. Boynton continued in these positions until 1961, and she also served as member and twice as president of the Minnesota State Board of Health between 1939 and 1961.

Boynton's widespread interest in public health was reflected not just in her health service leadership, but in her publication of more than 85 articles and several books on student health, defense worker's health, tuberculosis and menstrual problems.

During World War II, Dr. Boynton served as acting director of the University's School of Public Health. Immediately after the war, the space and staff of the Health Service, as well as the rest of the University, were strained by the great enrollment bulge. Plans were made for a new Health Service building which opened in the fall of 1950; this building was renamed the Boynton Health Service in 1975.

COMSTOCK HALL
210 Delaware Street SE,
University of Minnesota
Minneapolis, MN 55455

Ada Louise Comstock, for whom this residence hall was named, was born in 1876 in Moorhead. After graduating from high school at age 15, she began her higher education at the University of Minnesota in 1892, then transferred in 1894 to Smith College. Comstock did graduate work at Columbia University, where she received a master's degree in English, history and education in 1899. That year she returned to Minnesota and became an assistant, at $25 a month, in Professor Maria Sanford's Department of Rhetoric.

Comstock's contact with women students in her classes made her aware of their circumstances at the University; in contrast to her student years at the University when she lived at the home of the dean of the Law School, most female students lived anywhere they could find and were not a part of the University's extracurricular activities. The needs of the growing numbers of female students, 1000 of whom had signed a petition requesting an advocate, were recognized when thirty-one-year-old Ada Comstock was appointed the first Dean of Women at the University in 1907.

In order to develop a list of approved residences for women, the new Dean of Women visited boarding houses near the campus. Among criteria for approval were that residences be limited to female boarders and that a special room be designated a visiting room for callers. She also conducted a study of the effect of employment upon academic performance by women students; Comstock found that the grades of those who worked were as good as those not employed. Further evidence of her concern for student welfare can be found in her assistance to students who formed a cap and gown society and who gave teas in "promoting a spirit of sociability," and in the fact that she looked for jobs for women students during the 1911-12 Christmas vacation.

In pursuing her conviction that the University was responsible for students' intellectual attainment plus their physical well-being, Dean Comstock requested that a women's building, to replace the mice-infested "Ladies Parlor" in Old Main, be built. The money for the building was not provided by the University, but was donated by Thomas H. Shevlin, lumberman and manufacturer. In 1906 **Shevlin Hall** was completed and named for Alice Shevlin, the donor's wife. Thus a new era for women on campus was begun.

In 1912 Ada Comstock left the University to become Dean of Smith College, where her first project was evaluation of student housing and cost of expenses for a Smith student. Within five years, she had expanded available campus housing and proposed plans for regulating campus housing.

Dean Comstock spoke and wrote to inculcate in young women self-respect and the value of knowing how to employ oneself. She wrote a pamphlet at Smith describing vocations available to women, and she believed a college-educated woman had a responsibility to contribute to world welfare and amity among nations.

Comstock performed presidential duties when the presidency of Smith became vacant in 1917, but she was not named acting president, nor was she chosen to fill the position. In 1923 she was offered the first full-time presidency of Radcliffe College. When she was forty-seven years old, Ada Comstock assumed the challenging position at Radcliffe: the college did not have its own faculty, its finances and physical facilities were not in good shape, and, worst of all, Harvard President Abbott Lawrence Lowell seemed determined to cut the "Radcliffe parasite away from Harvard."

In seeking to handle this situation, Comstock proposed and persuaded the Radcliffe Associates and the Fellows of Harvard to accept a plan of joint appointments made possible by endowment money from Radcliffe. Radcliffe grew academically, and in the late 1930s offered a graduate course in music by visiting lecturer Nadia Boulanger to which any "properly qualified Harvard students" could be accepted.

More women instructors and students appeared at Radcliffe and Harvard during World War II. With Harvard's acceptance of classroom coeducation in 1943, Ada Comstock retired, her goal complete.

During the time of her presidency she was appointed by President Hoover to the National Commission on Law Observance and Enforcement, chaired by George Wickersham. The "Wickersham" Commission was charged with analyzing the entire federal judicial system and the problems of law enforcement with particular attention to the enforcement of Prohibition. Comstock also served in 1931 as a delegate to the Institute of Pacific Relations. After retirement, she became a Smith College Trustee and worked on plans for Radcliffe's graduate center.

By the time of her death in 1973, Ada Comstock had received fourteen honorary degrees and had three residence halls named for her. The Radcliffe College Alumnae Fund endowed a scholarship in her name, she received the Radcliffe Founders' Award, and she was cited as the "chief architect of the greatness of Radcliffe." Rockford College gave Ada Comstock its Jane Addams Medal and Ida M. Tarbell called her "one of the foremost women of the United States."

WORKING WOMEN
TOUR

North Star Woolen Mill, interior view, about 1905

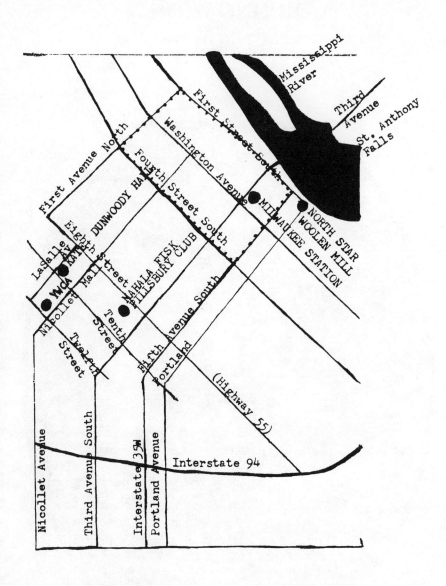

one inch equals
approx. 1/3 mile

GATEWAY

MILWAUKEE STATION/TRAVELERS AID
Third and Washington Avenues South
Minneapolis, MN 55401

For most of the young women arriving in Minneapolis in search of employment in the last quarter of the nineteenth century, the first sight of the city was the Gateway District. The railway stations, including the Milwaukee Depot which was built in 1899, were located in the heart of the Gateway. Even before the area had declined into a skid row in the twentieth century, there was concern that young women arriving alone in the city might be led astray by their ignorance and confusion. Labor recruitment offices for railway workers and farm hands were located near the railway stations, so unemployed men loitered in the area. Furthermore, the women arriving alone were in need of information: where to lodge, how to get around in the city, and how to go about seeking employment.

In an effort to aid these transient women, the YWCA and Woman's Christian Association of Minneapolis cooperated in 1893 to form a Travelers Aid Service. The two organizations sponsored matrons who would meet incoming trains and provide assistance to women, children, and the elderly.

One of the duties of the Travelers Aid matrons was to send away "mashers," described by Theodore Dreiser in *Sister Carrie* as men "whose dress or manners are calculated to elicit the admiration of susceptible young women." A Travelers Aid president was less charitable in her definition of a masher as "a certain species of animal which, for the lack of more manly employment, hangs around such places as railway stations, in the hope of entering upon a more or less harmful flirtation with waiting girls."

Besides sending away mashers, the Travelers Aid matrons bought train tickets for stranded persons and sent "girls adrift" to churches or rescue homes. One Aid matron arranged social afternoons for girls who were in domestic service. In 1910, the Minnesota Bureau of Labor estimated that more than 100 unescorted women passed daily through the Minneapolis railroad depot; by 1915, there were five Travelers Aid matrons working in the city's train depots.

Travelers Aid helped young women who were locating in the city by maintaining a list of places where they could find room and board and by operating an employment service in conjunction with the YWCA. Rooms for transients were maintained across from the Milwaukee Station, and in 1909 a Transient Home was opened at 724 South Third Avenue where lodgers could stay for up to two weeks for fifteen to fifty cents nightly. The YWCA funded the depot matrons while the WCA housed the transients. In 1916, the WCA established the Woman's Hotel at 122 Hennepin Avenue near the Great Northern Depot. During just nine months of its first year of existence, more than 4500 women and children stayed at the hotel, which was one of the first of its kind in the United States.

In 1932, the YWCA and Woman's Christian Association turned their work over to the National Travelers Aid Association, which continued to assist travelers at local railway and bus stations, and later at the airport, into the 1960s.

GATEWAY/PROSTITUTION

The area of Minneapolis known as the Gateway extends along the Mississippi River from First Avenue North to Fifth Avenue South and Fourth Street to First Street. From the 1870s until the turn of the century the Gateway was the heart of the city; this is where the first houses and businesses in Minneapolis were located. As the city grew, however, the shopping district and businesses moved to Nicollet Avenue and construction in the Gateway declined. Where banks, restaurants, and drugstores had thrived, mostly saloons, warehouses, factories, and labor recruitment offices remained. An 1884 ordinance contributed to the eventual decline of the Gateway; it set patrol limits which resulted in heavy concentration of saloons in areas like the Gateway where hard liquor was allowed.

Prostitution also flourished in the Gateway. Until 1910 the "social evil" was tolerated in certain segregated districts of the city, such as First Street. An indirect, quasi-legal license system was instituted in the 1870s whereby keepers of brothels would come into Municipal Court once a month and plead guilty to the charge of keeping a house of ill fame. At first the fine was fifty dollars plus five or ten dollars for each "inmate"; in 1897, the fine was raised to one hundred dollars and fining of inmates was discontinued.

The fines collected from prostitution in 1900 brought the city a revenue of $41,000, even though the police were not thorough in bringing prostitutes into court. It was estimated that there were 150 generally-recognized houses of prostitution in the city at that time, including some operating under the guise of candy stores.

In April 1910, Mayor James C. Haynes of Minneapolis ordered all red light districts closed and all "vicious women" (that is, prostitutes) excluded from saloons. The resulting controversy led to the appointment of a vice commission to study the situation and make a recommendation to Mayor Haynes. In its report, presented to the mayor in 1911, the commission urged that the ordinance against prostitution be strictly enforced.

Though the crackdown in 1910-11 may have reduced the number of brothels, or at least forced them to operate clandestinely, prostitution was by no means eliminated in Minneapolis. A study of prostitution and sex delinquency in Minneapolis made by the American Social Hygiene Association in 1939, found that all forms of prostitution were present and easily available in the city. Many of the prostitutes were controlled by a syndicate of brothel owners; each owner made monthly payments of fifty or sixty dollars which were pooled and allegedly distributed by a city official "where it would do the most good" (such as homes for work in the "care and reformation of fallen women"). According to the local underworld, Minneapolis was a "little Chicago," a wide open city, and the law enforcement officials were among those who profited from the system.

NORTH STAR WOOLEN MILL
South First Street and Portland Avenue
Minneapolis, MN 55401

In the last quarter of the nineteenth century thousands of young women began arriving in the Twin Cities in search of employment. Many were the daughters of farmers from outstate Minnesota or neighboring states. Rural areas held fewer employment oppportunities for women, so they came to the cities to work in factories, mills, stores, offices, and as domestic servants.

One of the primary employers of women, in Minneapolis as in eastern cities, was the garment industry. New Englanders who settled in Minneapolis hoped to make this a major center for textile manufacturing, and as a result a number of mills were constructed in the 1860s. But these mills catered to the homespun market, and as ready-made clothes from the East gained popularity, local manufacturers found it increasingly difficult to compete. By 1885 only one textile mill remained at St. Anthony Falls. This was the North Star Woolen Mill, built in 1864. Its success rested on the fact that in 1925 North Star was the principal woolen blanket mill in the United States, employing 270 persons. (The Pullman Palace Car Company used only North Star blankets in its railroad sleeping cars.) Though the building was extensively remodeled in 1925, the three-story section at South First Street and Portland Avenue dates from 1890 and can thus provide us with some idea of the atmosphere in which young women worked.

Eva McDonald described working conditions in the North Star Woolen Mill in her Eva Gay column in the *St. Paul Globe* on May 20, 1888. On a visit to the Mill, Eva Gay found that conditions varied widely from one department to another and that workers in one department often knew nothing about work and wages in another department. The worst conditions were in the basement of the old part of the Mill, where washing and drying of blankets and flannels was done. The room was dimly lit, the heat from the washing and drying machines intense, about 98 degrees, and the floor was dirty. Some girls worked on heavy machines called "gigs"; others were engaged in "bushing," or picking specks off the blankets. The girls who worked in the washing and drying room thought that girls in other departments looked down on them for working in such a dirty place.

The workroom in the basement of the newer part of the building showed a marked contrast to the washing and drying room. This room was well lit, clean and cool, and was arranged so that girls could sit while they finished and pressed the blankets. In the weaving room on the second floor, however, the girls had to stand at their looms for ten hours a day. The noise of the eighty-three looms was deafening. Eva Gay was impressed by the extreme cleanliness of the weaving room until she learned from the girls that they had to clean their machines and "sweep and fix up the place neat and tidy" during their noon-hour breaks so that visitors to the Mill would comment on the pleasant working conditions. There were plenty of windows in the weaving room, but all of them were closed to avoid causing the girls colds by the drafts. Therefore, the air was "warm and close everywhere and in some places the smell of the wool was disagreeable." Most of the girls who worked at the Mill made 90¢ a day, a few $1.35. But it took four or five years to become proficient enough to make the higher wage and few girls could last that long in the Mill. Most could not work year round, but had to take time off in order to rest because the Mill work was so demanding.

WOMEN WORKERS

The many young women who came to Minneapolis in the late nineteenth century to work in factories and shops found it difficult to support themselves on their meager wages. The average woman worker in the 1880s earned three or four dollars a week, but the Bureau of Labor estimated that the cost of living for a female boarder was six dollars per week. Some of the women workers lived at home with their families; others lived alone or with friends in apartments or boarding houses. The number of boarding houses or other affordable accommodations was not sufficient to house all the women workers, as is evident in articles which appeared in the Minneapolis and St. Paul newspapers in the late 1880s. In April 1888, a writer in the *Minneapolis Journal* deplored the poor wages and working conditions of female workers in the city; another article proposed that an inexpensive boarding house for women be established.

Later that month 250 women who worked sewing overalls and jumpers at the Shotwell, Clerihew, and Lothman Dry Goods Factory, located at 101-106 South Second, went on strike to protest a series of reductions in wages. The women workers were paid three cents per jumper and even the fastest workers found it difficult to make $3.00 or $3.50 per week. With a cost of living nearly double that amount, these workers could not sustain a cut in wages.

The factory remained idle for three weeks, during which time the firm refused to submit the case to arbitration. The striking workers received moral and financial support from various labor organizations, including a pledge from working men that they would not wear clothes made by the company. The strikers determined that if the company continued to reject their pleas for fair wages they would seek work elsewhere. By mid-June, however, many of the workers had returned to work on the company's terms. The workers ultimately won a bittersweet victory: the company went bankrupt in July, 1888.

A young journalist, Eva McDonald (1866-1956) attended several of the strike meetings and reported on the strike for the *St. Paul Globe*. Earlier that year she had written a series of articles on women workers in the Twin Cities for the *Globe*. McDonald, who had previously done proofreading and typesetting for a local newspaper, visited print shops, book binderies, steam laundries, woolen mills, garment and shoe factories, and other establishments that employed women. She often posed as a worker in order to gather information from suspicious employers and reticent workers. McDonald's first article appeared in March, 1888 under the pen name "Eva Gay," and the series continued for nearly a year.

John McGaughey, an organizer and national officer of the Knights of Labor, heard McDonald speaking in support of the Shotwell, Clerihew, and Lothman strikers. Impressed by her fluency, he set out to train her as an orator and labor agitator and she attended various labor meetings with McGaughey.

In the fall of 1888, McDonald was nominated by the Democratic party to run for the Minneapolis School Board—the first woman in Hennepin County to run for the Board. Though she received a high vote count, she lost in an election that went heavily Republican.

In April, 1889 McDonald was one of the many local women who were active in support of a strike of St. Paul streetcar workers. The women held meetings in sympathy with the strikers and visited those who had been arrested and were in jail. Maria Sanford, a University of Minnesota professor, persuaded a group of prominent men to call on Thomas Lowry, the owner of the streetcar company, to ask him to arbitrate the strike.

Eva McDonald expanded her labor-organizing efforts in 1889 by lecturing throughout the state for the Farmers' Alliance. She was well received by the farmers and also by their wives, who gathered around her after the lectures to question her about factory conditions; many of these women had daughters working in the Cities.

Among McDonald's other labor-related activities was membership in the Eight Hour League, an organization endeavoring to reduce the length of the workday. From the back of her father's wagon she gave speeches in support of the League's efforts. In 1891 she married Frank Valesh, the first president of the Minnesota Federation of Labor. Eva Valesh was labor editor for the *Minneapolis Tribune* from 1892 to 1894 and in 1893 she edited the *St. Paul Trades and Labor Assembly Bulletin.* She left Minnesota in 1894 to live on the East Coast, where she first wrote for the *New York Journal* and later was asked by Samuel Gompers to be coeditor of the *American Federationist.* Eva Valesh worked with Gompers for eight years and afterwards continued to edit, in addition to her involvement in charitable and relief work. She was employed by the *New York Times* as a proofreader for many years, retiring in 1951 at the age of 85. Valesh died in 1956.

Few women in the Twin Cities were as active in organized labor as Eva McDonald Valesh. The involvement of women increased over the years, however. By 1901 a bindery girls' union, a garment workers' union, and a dressmakers' union had been established with women as officers. A waitresses' union was founded soon after 1901.

Women also played a significant role in the labor unrest of the 1930s in Minneapolis. During the Teamster Strike of 1934, members of the Women's Auxiliary answered phones, prepared food at strike headquarters (sometimes making as many as 15,000 meals a day!), collected public donations to help support the strikers, and sold copies of the daily strike bulletin. They also cared for injured strikers at a first aid station so that the strikers would not have to be taken to hospitals, where they were often arrested. Perhaps most impressive was a march on city hall by 700 members of the women's auxiliary to protest the actions of police during the strike.

Women were more directly involved in the 1935-36 strike at the Strutwear Knitting Company in Minneapolis, where the majority of workers were female. Previous attempts to organize the plant had been unsuccessful because of the employer's use of yellow dog contracts and lockouts of union members, but by the end of the strike almost all workers belonged to the union. While men retained leadership and organizing positions in this strike, women workers picketed and distributed handbills throughout the eight months of the strike. The company's owner finally conceded to the workers' demands for union recognition and adjustment of wages to a level commensurate with other knitting plants in the Midwest.

KATE DUNWOODY HALL
52 South Tenth Street
Minneapolis, MN 55403

MAHALA FISK PILLSBURY CLUB
819 Second Avenue South
Minneapolis, MN 55402

Women who had migrated because of the need to find work, independence and excitement in the growing cities of St. Paul and Minneapolis often had difficulty finding decent, and affordable places to live. Traditionally, women were expected to live with their families until they married, but in the years after the Civil War, women found jobs as dressmakers, milliners, teachers, waitresses, domestic servants, and in other typical female occupations in cities. By 1900, almost half of Minneapolis' female labor force lived apart from their families; this migration of young women created a demand for accommodations at boarding houses and women's hotels.

Two disadvantages hampered women from finding decent, affordable housing. According to Eva McDonald, who published a series of articles in 1888 in the *St. Paul Globe* about Minneapolis working women, many landlords were unwilling to rent to women because they believed women gossiped, demanded extra attention, and because they thought female tenants lowered the respectability of their lodgings. Minneapolis women workers also earned extremely low wages; that the average woman worker in Minneapolis in the 1880s earned from $3 to $4 a week was supported by the assumption that women were working outside their proper sphere of domesticity in order to buy luxuries or for "pin money" and were housed with their parents. But the fact was that many women fed, clothed, and sheltered themselves at the cost of about $6 a week. Thus it was in the dingiest, most crowded districts of the Twin Cities, near the "wicked" dance halls and houses of prostitution that working women found the cheapest housing at $2.50 to $3.50 per week.

Because their financial circumstances cast women into poor living conditions, concern about morals and the problems of "women adrift" arose in the late nineteenth century, and "Purity Crusades" were launched in many cities. Supervision of housing for working women so that they lived with "home-like" rules and regulations and morality and knew the difference between vice and virtue was part of the "Purity Crusades." In the opinion of such nineteenth century crusaders and those interested in "humanity and the morals of society," women workers' low wages and separation from the mores and values of domesticity set them too close to prostitution.

Concern about the moral purity of working women and their need for safe and wholesome housing and protection led to the establishment of supervised boarding clubs, substitute domestic environments for women throughout the United States. By 1889, about ninety such boarding clubs had been started by the YWCAs and Woman's Christian Associations of various cities.

The first such club in Minneapolis was the Woman's Boarding Home, established by the Woman's Christian Association in a small downtown house in 1874. In 1878 the home moved to a large, three-story house which had registered 1400 women by 1883. A second club, the "Branch," intended for poorer women, opened in 1885. Between 1900 and 1928 eight more boarding homes were established in Minneapolis by the Association. Because many women were working during World War I, the decade of 1910 to 1920 was the peak of the boarding club movement.

Some of the clubs were funded by gifts. Former Governor John S. Pillsbury donated a house to replace the Branch. The house at 819 Second Avenue South, was named for his wife, Mahala Fisk Pillsbury; it operates today, in the same location, as the eight-story **Mahala Fisk Pillsbury Club. Kate Dunwoody Hall** was built in 1965 to replace the William H. Dunwoody Residence that had been given in 1905 to the Woman's Christian Association to serve as the Woman's Boarding Home.

YWCA
1130 Nicollet Avenue
Minneapolis, MN 55403

The Minneapolis Young Women's Christian Association was organized in 1891 by a small group of business women who were members of the Christian Endeavor Societies of a number of churches in the city. These women banded together to do interdenominational work and to promote Christian culture among themselves; they wished to have frequent meetings and needed a central meeting place.

The first site of the YWCA was a second-story flat at 45 Eighth Street South. Gym classes (called "physical culture") were held in the vestry of the Plymouth Church at Nicollet and Eighth Street, because the flat was too small to accommodate these classes. When new quarters were occupied a year later, a long narrow hall was used for gym classes and as a dining room. Hot and cold drinks were served out of a tiny kitchen and soup was sold for three cents a cup. The YWCA was housed in several locations before settling at this site in 1929, with this new building completed in 1976.

The YWCA programs in the early years ranged from cooking, dressmaking, literature, and language classes to bicycle clubs, rowing, and basketball. A summer camp for young working women was started in 1908. It was held first at Lake Calhoun and later at Lyman Lodge on Lake Minnetonka.

The YWCA also attempted to aid women seeking employment and housing in Minneapolis, often in cooperation with the Woman's Christian Association; an employment bureau was operated from the earliest years of the YWCA until 1952.

Concern for working women prompted YWCA officials to conduct a survey of women employed in Minneapolis in 1898. The survey revealed that about 1000 women and girls were employed in the offices, stores, mills, and factories within a six block radius of Washington Avenue and First Avenue North. Subsequently, the YWCA formed an extension department to work with women in industry and business, and in 1900 a north branch of the YWCA was opened in this area. The branch was intended as a meeting place for working women and its cafeteria provided hot meals instead of "cold lunches eaten at desk or machine."

The YWCA also offered noon programs at factories to help the workers relax and to attract new members to the organization. Although amenities were lacking at the typical factories and sweatshops, these YWCA programs had their effect on some employers, as well as workers. Bemis Brothers Bag Company put in lunch and rest rooms for female workers at the factory. Cream of Wheat followed this example when a new plant was built by buying a piano so employees could have music programs at noon.

DOWNTOWN MINNEAPOLIS
WALKING TOUR

Young Quinlan Store, about 1908

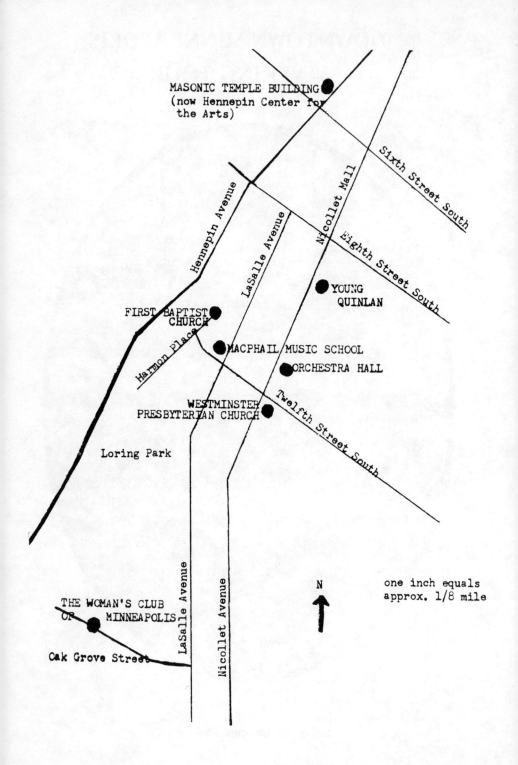

MASONIC TEMPLE BUILDING
(now Hennepin Center for
the Arts)

Sixth Street South

Hennepin Avenue

LaSalle Avenue

Nicollet Mall

Eighth Street South

YOUNG
QUINLAN

FIRST BAPTIST
CHURCH

Harmon Place

MACPHAIL MUSIC SCHOOL

ORCHESTRA HALL

WESTMINSTER
PRESBYTERIAN CHURCH

Twelfth Street South

Loring Park

N

one inch equals
approx. 1/8 mile

LaSalle Avenue

Nicollet Avenue

THE WOMAN'S CLUB
OF MINNEAPOLIS

Oak Grove Street

58

WESTMINSTER PRESBYTERIAN CHURCH/
WOMAN'S CHRISTIAN TEMPERANCE UNION
12th Street and Nicollet Avenue
Minneapolis, MN 55403

The Minnesota State Woman's Christian Temperance Union was founded in Westminster Presbyterian Church in September, 1877, three years after the National Union, and two years after the St. Paul Union, were started.

The fast, almost spontaneous, organization of the national WCTU at a time when organization of women was unusual, was called the "whirlwind of the Lord" as the nation became temperance-minded within about six months in 1873 and 1874.

The WCTU objective was "to carry forward measures which with the blessing of God, will result in promoting the cause of total abstinence and in outlawing liquor traffic." Saloons and taverns were chosen as targets for WCTU marches because they were seen as disruptive to the social institutions of home and church; it was believed that the best way to eliminate human misery would be to eliminate liquor. At the height of WCTU power, 45 years after the organization's founding and just before the passage of the Eighteenth Amendment, the watchwords became "educate, agitate and organize" as civil rights for women, labor unionism and international peace, as well as temperance, were targets. Although women were doused with beer thrown from second-floor windows while they prayed on the sidewalks near saloons, after about 1900 there was no more marching on taverns, except for that done by Carrie Nation, who never was a WCTU member.

Early organization of the WCTU in Minnesota was by congressional districts, each district president becoming a state vice president. At the first convention of the state group, 32 local temperance organizations were represented. The work of the WCTU was carried on by 24 departments, each with a state superintendent and a local superintendent. Among these departments were prevention, Americanization, medical temperance, Sunday school, scientific temperance instruction, penal and reformatory, Scandinavian, anti-narcotics, and Evangelistic work among woodsmen, soldiers, sailors, firemen and miners.

After its founding, the state WCTU held annual meetings with temperance regarded as the most important reform among many. Its members, identified by white ribbon bows which were their membership badges, were fighters in other battles, including suffrage. Although there is scarcely a community in the nation that has not felt the direct or indirect influence of the WCTU, the record of accomplishments in Minneapolis is impressive. They include: the first curfew ordinance; first free kindergarten; salary paid for first matron of jails and first cooking teacher in the public schools; first law requiring teaching of effects of alcohol; measures against white slave traffic, and in favor of raising the age of consent from 7 to 18; operation of a home for unwed mothers; aid to immigrants; a rest cottage at the State Fair; support of French orphans during World War I; newsboys' evening school; lunch room for working women; food served to firemen at fires; ice water barrels on street corners during summer months; sponsorship of many temperance essay contests; opposition to military training in public schools, and thousands of signatures procured to petition for limitation of armaments.

The fulfillment of WCTU hopes came in 1920 with Prohibition. But since the repeal of Prohibition in 1933, character-building and an educational campaign among the young against the alcoholic menace have been stressed. WCTU membership has declined, and the temperance cause was further harmed in the early 1970s when official ages of adulthood were lowered. The years of WCTU as the only woman's organization made up of members of all denominations doing religious and reform work, and days of WCTU strength when women were visibly active in political and social efforts long before their enfranchisement, were fading.

MASONIC TEMPLE BUILDING (now Hennepin Center for the Arts)
528 Hennepin Avenue   Minneapolis, MN 55403
FIRST BAPTIST CHURCH / WOMAN SUFFRAGE
1020 Harmon Place   Minneapolis, MN 55403

Efforts in behalf of woman suffrage and rights for women began early in Minnesota. Harriet Bishop addressed small parlor gatherings of women in 1847 in St. Paul, and lectures on the subject were given in the late 1850s and early 1860s. In 1866 women began petitioning the legislature for an amendment to the State Constitution that would strike the word "male" from the suffrage clause. The early bill that called for such an amendment received few votes and much ridicule; this ridicule energized supporters to greater efforts in securing petitions, resolutions, hearings, and organizing suffrage clubs.

Organization toward suffrage occurred where there were strong leaders; thus it happened that the first suffrage societies in Minnesota, formed in 1869, were in Minneapolis, Kasson, Rochester, and Champlin. The state woman's suffrage association, affiliated with the National American Woman Suffrage Association, functioned actively from its founding in 1881 until 1919, when the vote was won.

One of the first successes of the Minnesota suffragists came in 1875 when the legislature passed a law allowing women over the age of twenty-one to vote in school elections. Suffragists attributed this victory to the fact that they had not agitated the issue, and the wording of the amendment was such that those who did not cast a vote on the resolution were in effect voting for it. Another small victory came in 1885 when women were granted the right to vote in matters concerning public libraries.

Suffragists presented pro-suffrage petitions with thousands of signatures to the legislature each year from 1890 to 1896. Political Equality Clubs were organized in the 1890s in both St. Paul and Minneapolis. About 1897 the Minneapolis Club gained wider acceptance when a group of local women physicians (Drs. Cora Smith Eaton, Ethel E. Hurd, Annah Hurd, Bessie Parke Haines, and Margaret Koch) became active in state and local suffrage work. The Minneapolis Political Equality Club had its headquarters in the reception room of the offices of Drs. Eaton and Koch on the sixth and seventh floors of the **Masonic Temple Building**. The Political Action Club of Minneapolis sought to educate the public about woman's suffrage and to elect women to school and library boards.

Also in 1897, the conference of the officers of the National American Woman Suffrage Association was held in Minneapolis at the **First Baptist Church**. Compared with today's cavernous convention centers, First Baptist Church may seem rather modest. Yet, as the largest hall in Minneapolis around the turn of the century, this church was often used for conventions.

Four years later, in 1901, the national convention of the Suffrage Association assembled here at First Baptist Church, during the last week of May and the first week of June. Susan B. Anthony, Anna Howard Shaw, Alice Stone Blackwell, and Carrie Chapman Catt were among the thousands attending, with Catt presiding in place of Anthony for the first time.

In the early 1900s, suffrage continued to be the butt of ridicule from the press and many men and women, but with the growth of Political Equality Clubs, independent suffrage clubs, the idea of economic independence for women, and the Minnesota Equal Franchise League (its work included county and legislative district organization to broaden the work of national suffrage), suffrage sentiment made some gains. Also, after 1900, when suffrage became linked with principles of progressivism, prohibition, civic reform, and protective laws for workers, gains were made.

Two thousand men and women participated in the 1914 suffrage parade in Minneapolis; the following year the National Woman's party, Minnesota Branch, was organized to secure a national suffrage amendment. Open air and indoor meetings, suffrage literature in doctors' offices, a speakers' bureau, automobile touring campaigns, participation in the 1916-1918 national campaigns, a suffrage Red Cross unit, and an appeal by Carrie Chapman Catt not to abandon suffrage for war work (because she thought the vote was needed more than ever during war) marked suffrage activity in the years directly preceding its passage. Support also came from male friends of suffrage with Minnesota legislatures becoming more favorable at each session until 1917, when both houses were ready to submit any bills requested by the Minnesota Suffrage Association Board. Minnesota Governor J.A.A. Burnquist telegraphed to all governors whose states had not acted upon the suffrage amendment to join with him in 1920 in calling special sessions of their legislatures to ratify the national suffrage amendment. The Federal Amendment was considered at a special session of the Minnesota legislature; it passed both houses with few dissenting votes, amidst laughter, cheers, and the waving of suffrage flags.

YOUNG QUINLAN
901 Nicollet Mall (Avenue)
Minneapolis, MN 55402

While most female workers in the Twin Cities in the late nineteenth century were employed in domestic service or factory work, there were some exceptions. One was Elizabeth Quinlan, who started her retail career at age nine clerking in her father's grocery store, and, to help support their large family, at age sixteen clerked for $10 a week in Goodfellow's Department Store on Nicollet Avenue; Goodfellow's carried heavy woolen and cotton union suits, racks of calico, Mother Hubbards, stiff petticoats of drill or corded sateen and a few tailored suits.

Quinlan wished to own a store that would carry ready-to-wear garments for women, which were at the time practically unheard-of in Minnesota. Nicollet Avenue was gas-lighted and paved with red bumpy cedar blocks in 1894 when she and Fred

Young, a fellow clerk at Goodfellow's, opened a small shop in the back of a building at 513 Nicollet Avenue. In this day of home sewing with coats and suits made by dressmakers and tailors, Young and Quinlan imported gowns from Chicago, New York, and Paris to create the second specialty shop in the nation to house several departments, each carrying a different kind of apparel, so that women could buy everything they needed in one store.

Fred Young managed the finances of the store, while Quinlan was in charge of purchasing, sales, and advertising—the only woman merchandise buyer in the United States at the time. Young became ill soon after the store was opened, however, leaving the total responsibility of running the business to Quinlan. Because there were no training schools for this sort of thing, she learned about the business by seeking audiences with other merchants, such as Paul Bonwit and Horace Saks, and by studying the gowns at the June races in Paris, where world-renowned fashion shows were held. Thus, in place of union suits, Quinlan sold fur- and lace-trimmed negliges, imported gowns and ermine wraps, and she created an exclusive shop for "ladies' ready-to-wear," a model for other women's apparel stores, so that visitors to Minneapolis in the early 1900s often wanted to see two places—Minnehaha Falls and Young Quinlan.

Quinlan's business continued to do almost as well in later years as the day the store first opened, when the merchandise was nearly all sold within three hours. This store, at 901 Nicollet, was designed by New York architect Frederick Ackerman and built in 1926-27. A grand staircase, antique amber cathedral windows, handmade walnut wood display cases, and hand-wrought iron grillwork gave the store a five million dollar construction price.

Elizabeth Quinlan conducted her 51-year retail business career guided by principles such as: treat the public well, give them a square deal and they will return the treatment to you; maintain personal contact with customers; carry only merchandise that is well-made and a good value; do not sell cheap merchandise at sales; get discounts by paying bills within ten days; and employ intelligent, knowledgeable personnel responsible for the buying and sales of each of the eighteen specialty departments.

The pioneer retailer, who designed her own ads in the evening and took them to the newspaper around midnight, received many honors before her death in 1947. In 1935, Fortune Magazine cited Quinlan as one of 16 outstanding women executives and the foremost women's specialty shop executive in the country. She was the only woman on the advisory board of the National Recovery Administration. She was the only Minneapolis woman selected for the March of Time film, "The Most Distinguished Business Women of US," and in 1937, the Women's National Press Club named her the outstanding woman executive.

Elizabeth Quinlan had offers to work elsewhere but she chose Minneapolis; she participated in civic and philanthropic activities, guaranteed many theatrical performances, and once served as director of a taxi cab company because she wanted taxi service for women and children to be as safe as the streetcar system. Minneapolis, in turn, honored her in 1940 as its most distinguished and best-known woman.

ORCHESTRA HALL
1111 Nicollet Avenue
Minneapolis, MN 55403

Minneapolis women's involvement in the arts began early and created lasting monuments to the culture of the area. The Minneapolis Society of Fine Arts was incorporated in January, 1883, with large credit for its organization and promotion given to women; the Ladies' Thursday Musical, one of the oldest clubs in the state, was founded in 1892 to develop and encourage musical talent among Minneapolis women, and to sponsor new compositions in addition to recitals by well-known artists. Although music had been taught in the Minneapolis Public Schools since the Civil War, Thursday Musical members, who numbered 500 in 1900, gave programs and encouraged study of music in the schools to the extent that by the 1920s vocal music was required of every pupil from kindergarten through tenth grade, and high school graduates had sung at least four of five "great choral classics," such as the *Messiah*. Ladies' Thursday Musical members helped to establish the Department of Music at the University, created scholarship funds for talented girls, and provided thousands of music lessons at ten cents each in city settlement houses and rescue homes.

Minneapolis distinguished itself in 1903 when it became one of seven cities with a major orchestra. The Minnesota Orchestra, for which **Orchestra Hall** was built in 1974, had its origins as the Minneapolis Symphony when the city ranked eighteenth among US cities in population.

The Minneapolis Symphony owes its conception to Anna Eugenia Schoen-Rene. Schoen-Rene came to Minneapolis from Paris in 1893 following preparation for an operatic career. She weighed 98 pounds upon her arrival to visit her sister and recuperate from what doctors called a hopeless case of consumption; in spite of her poor health, Schoen-Rene gave a public recital within three months and, in her words, "started the University's music department" when she organized the University Choral Union as an amalgamation of student glee clubs during her first year in Minneapolis.

In 1898 Schoen-Rene was credited with being the first woman orchestral conductor in the country when she organized a chamber orchestra and decided to establish a full-scale professional symphony orchestra. As a promotor of musical culture and performances, Schoen-Rene's efforts to raise the city's musical standards by the "scruff of the neck" included organizing festivals and contracting singers, violinists, pianists, opera companies, and orchestras, and signing bushels of passes if advance sales to a performance were poor. Schoen-Rene's enterprise was rewarded when the Minneapolis Symphony was founded—by others, when she was out of town. Later, as an instructor of voice at Julliard School of Music, Schoen-Rene's reputation was well-known, and she counted Risë Stevens among her students there.

In 1911, when the Minneapolis Symphony was only eight years old, a group of women, impressed with a concert for young people in New York, organized the Young People's Symphony Association to give all local children the opportunity to hear the Symphony. The Minneapolis Board of Education, and after 1930, the PTA, underwrote ticket sales, and Minneapolis Schools incorporated concert attendance into the fifth and sixth grade music curriculum. The first concert, November 24, 1911, at the Eleventh Street Auditorium (later The Lyceum Theater) sold out to the first thirteen schools of 72 that applied for tickets, so the concert had to be given again on November 27. Ticket prices ranged from ten to fifty cents, although the Free Seat and Transportation Fund was organized so all students could attend.

The concerts were eventually moved to the larger seating capacity of Northrup Auditorium and through the years pre-concert recordings, tapes, television shows, and other lessons have been used to add to the educational value of the concerts. A project, first called Symphony Art and later Visual Music, encouraged students to draw and paint their reactions to the music of the orchestra. Auditions for instrumentalists of high school age to solo with the orchestra at Young People's Concerts were also added to Young People's Association undertakings. The various Minneapolis Symphony and Minnesota Orchestra conductors led programs attended by two million youngsters during the first sixty years of the Association, supporting a cause-effect relationship between the Young People's Symphony Association and the later enthusiasm of adult concert-goers.

Minneapolis was further established as a leader in children's music when Ruth Anderson, of the MacPhail Music School faculty, started children's orchestras in the Minneapolis Public Schools. In 1923 she directed a children's orchestra of 1000 members, and in 1924 there were 55 orchestras in Minneapolis grade and junior high schools under her supervision.

Northwestern National Life Insurance Company Auditorium, Wesley Methodist Church, First Baptist Church, Swedish Tabernacle, International Stock Food Auditorium, and The Lyceum Theater were the Minneapolis Symphony's early homes before Verna Golden Scott became the Symphony's manager in 1930. Scott, a violinist who studied in Leipzig with Hans Sitt, began her managerial work by arranging to bring to the University of Minnesota campus soloists and groups such as the Chicago Civic Opera, New York Theatre Guild, and Paul Whiteman's Band with George Gershwin at the piano. These concerts were so successful in sponsoring music at affordable prices for thousands of students that it was said Verna Scott accomplished one of the greatest cultural achievements in the history of the state. She was the music impresario who also arranged for the Boston Symphony to play in Minneapolis in 1929 as part of the dedication of Cyrus Northrup Memorial Auditorium.

In 1930 the Minneapolis Symphony desperately needed a new home because the rental for The Lyceum Theater had doubled and the Theater underwent some structural changes that made it less desirable as an orchestra hall.

Scott, as the second woman manager of a major American orchestra, engineered the partnership of the University and the Symphony that made Minnesota the only campus harboring a major professional orchestra as a permanent resident. The orchestra became a member of the academic faculty so that the Orchestral Association could continue its corporate existence, allowed to manage itself, yet having as its home the property of a state-supported institution, and the largest single-concert audience seating (Northrup Auditorium) of all major American orchestras. Verna Scott continued as Minneapolis Symphony manager until 1938; she worked with Maestros Henri Verbrugghen, Eugene Ormandy, and Dimitri Mitropoulos. Scott continued to manage the University Artists' Course until her retirement from the University in 1944.

In 1949, when Antal Dorati succeeded Mitropoulos as music director of the Symphony, the Women's Association of the Minneapolis Symphony Orchestra (WAMSO) was founded—but only after several years of lobbying to convince members of the Orchestral Association board that women should be organized to do supportive work for the orchestra. The Symphony's manager under Mitropoulos threatened to leave if women gained influence. Since the time of its organization, WAMSO has sponsored numerous educational, financial and performing projects. Young Audiences brings performing artists into schools while Young Artists Competition is for solo instrumentalists under age 26. The annual Symphony Ball, sales of *Encore* (a cookbook of favorite recipes of famous world musicians), a tennis tournament, and Twin City Tours have enabled WAMSO to bring additional income to the Minnesota Orchestral Association. WAMSO, whose home has now become Orchestra Hall, is the second largest organization of its kind in the nation.

THE WOMAN'S CLUB OF MINNEAPOLIS
410 Oak Grove Street
Minneapolis, MN 55403

The Woman's Club of Minneapolis celebrated its seventy-fifth anniversary in March of 1982. When the Club was organized in 1907 the purpose was "culture of its members and public service"; at the time of the seventy-five-year milestone, the aims of the Club remain much the same. Early Woman's Club projects were drives for sanitation in public schools, equipping and supporting playgrounds, and hiring visiting nurses for the public schools. The latter project was financed through Tag Day, when Club members collected money on street corners. The Club members also advocated water and milk pureness inspection in Minneapolis. More recently, the Club's public service goal has been met through the awarding of scholarships and financial contributions to Walker Art Center, Camp Courage, Phyllis Wheatley Community Center, Big Sister Association, and numerous other civic organizations. Restoration of the Ard Godfrey house was the Club's Bicentennial gift to Minneapolis. This house, the first frame house in St. Anthony, was built in 1848 by Godfrey, a millwright, with lumber from the first sawmill in the village. The Godfrey house is open to the public at Chute Square, Central and University Avenues.

The first meetings of the Woman's Club were held in a room above a downtown store. In 1913 the Club purchased the Rufus Rand home at 1526 Harmon Place to serve as a clubhouse. The Club soon outgrew this building, so in 1927 construction began at the Oak Grove site. The following year the present clubhouse was opened. It has been a center for fellowship, education, and civic enterprise through the years, and the clubhouse has also served as a residence for women. At the time of the fiftieth anniversary of the clubhouse, Lillian Nippert Zelle, who had been a member of the Club for 60 years, reminisced about plans for the building: "When we built the Club, we swore we were going to have an alley entrance for men. We felt it was fitting retaliation for the Minneapolis Club, where women were restricted to using the back door."

HEALTH CARE
TOUR

Maternity Hospital, original main building, about 1905

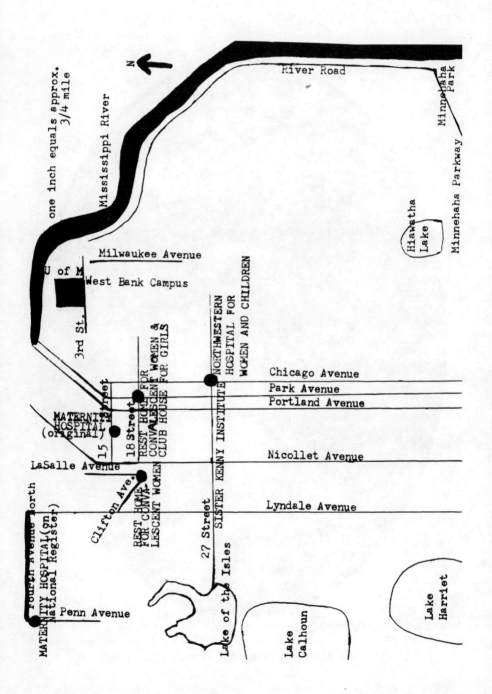

NORTHWESTERN HOSPITAL FOR WOMEN AND CHILDREN
27th Street and Chicago Avenue
Minneapolis, MN 55407

The rapid population growth of Minneapolis in the 1860s and 1870s was accompanied by a proliferation of disease. Due in part to advertisements touting Minnesota as an asylum for consumptives—the climate was thought to have a salutary effect—tuberculosis was the leading cause of death in Hennepin County, followed by such diseases as typhoid, dysentery, and pneumonia. Infant diseases ranked as the fourth largest cause of death. But not until 1871 was the first hospital established in Minneapolis. A second hospital was founded in 1881, and the two together could accommodate perhaps 150 patients.

Concerned about the inadequacy of facilities for the city's sick persons, a group of women headed by Harriet Walker (1841-1917) met at the Quaker Meeting House in November, 1882, to discuss the possibility of establishing a hospital for women and children. Once the decision to proceed had been made, the women lost no time, and in December Northwestern Hospital for Women and Children was opened in a rented house. A year later a lot at 26th Street and Clinton Avenue was purchased and a building constructed. The Hospital later moved to the Chicago Avenue location.

The Hospital was intended for medical, surgical, obstetrical, and gynecological cases and for diseased children. An early advertisement claimed that the facility offered "the advantages of a hospital combined with the comforts of a home." An average of thirty patients per month was cared for during the late 1880s. Priority was given to "charity patients" (those unable to pay), but patients who were charges of the city and paying patients were also admitted. Male patients were first received in the Hospital in 1900.

The Hospital was directed by a board of "lady managers" consisting the first year of sixty-three women and five honorary members, with Harriet Walker as president. Doctors Mary Whetstone and Mary Hood made up the first medical staff; they were soon joined by Dr. Emily Fifield and two assistants. A nurses' training school was also offered at the Hospital.

The Hospital is now part of the Abbott-Northwestern Hospital. One of the buildings is named for Harriet Walker, who served as president of the board of managers for Northwestern Hospital for Women and Children throughout her life.

MATERNITY HOSPITAL (former site)
316 East Fifteenth Street
Minneapolis, MN 55404

Born in Lowell, Vermont, in 1843, Martha Rogers moved with her family to Fort Atkinson, Iowa, at age four. Her parents, who were among the first white settlers in the Northwest Territory, were abolitionists and maintained a station on the underground railroad. Martha learned to live without luxuries so fugitive slaves would have food to eat.

During the Civil War, Martha Rogers taught school and raised funds for the United States Sanitary Commission. In 1867 she married William Ripley and moved to

Lawrence, Massachusetts, where her husband was manager of a paper mill. While in Lawrence, Martha Ripley successfully petitioned for the appointment of a police matron and was herself given the job. In 1875 she became involved in the woman suffrage movement. Meanwhile, illness in the mill towns had aroused her interest in the study of medicine and in 1880 she entered Boston University School of Medicine. She graduated in 1883, the same year her husband was severely injured in a mill accident. Because William Ripley had relatives in Minneapolis, they moved there, and Martha Ripley began a medical practice, specializing in obstetrics and children's diseases.

Very soon after her arrival in Minneapolis Dr. Ripley was elected President of the Minnesota Woman Suffrage Association. During five or six years as leader and later from the ranks, she sought to develop alliances with women who were organizing in support of temperance. Ripley's association with Lucy Stone and Henry Blackwell helped bring the seventeenth annual convention of the American Woman Suffrage Association to Minneapolis in 1885. Ripley's concern for women's welfare also prompted her to lobby to raise the age of consent for girls from ten to eighteen.

In November, 1886, aware of the need for a home for unmarried mothers, Ripley rented a five-room house at 316 East Fifteenth Street as a shelter for three of her patients. That was the beginning of Maternity Hospital. Within a month, the Hospital had outgrown these quarters and a larger house at 609 Eight and a Half Street North was provided free of rent by friends of Ripley's. The Hospital moved again in July, 1887, to a twenty-room house at 2529 Fourth Avenue South and in 1896 settled at its final location at Western and Penn Avenues North.

Ripley stressed social services as well as medical care for mothers—rich and poor, married and unmarried—and for indigent infants. Maternity was the first hospital in Minneapolis to have a separate social service department. The infant and maternal mortality rates of the Hospital were very low and the reputation of the Hospital was such that it attracted patients from distant cities.

Besides striving for better medical care, Ripley worked for other improvements in the lives of women and children. She fought for representation of women on the city school board, urged a single moral standard for men and women, and recommended incineration of garbage and cremation of the dead. In addition, she worked for the establishment of playgrounds, pure water, and better quarantine facilities.

Ripley served as head physician of Maternity Hospital until her death in 1915. The Hospital remained in existence until 1956. The building at Western and Penn, the only one of the Hospital's sites that is still extant, is listed on the National Register of Historic Places.

While she was busy with her medical practice and politics, Ripley's husband took care of their four children. William Ripley thought their daughters benefitted as his companions in fishing and other outdoor activities, and for the sake of their health, the Ripley daughters did not wear tightly-laced Victorian corsets.

In 1939 a memorial plaque was installed in the rotunda of the Minnesota State Capitol to honor Martha Ripley. It reads, "She was a champion of righteousness and justice who served humanity with farsighted vision and sympathy."

WOMEN'S WELFARE LEAGUE/
REST HOME FOR CONVALESCENT WOMEN
1801 Park Avenue
Minneapolis, MN 55404

The Women's Welfare League was organized in 1911 to promote the social welfare of women and girls. The League's first goal was to provide wholesome entertainment for young girls as a counter to public dance halls. The Minneapolis Vice Commission Report of 1911, which was concerned primarily with the problem of prostitution in the city, concluded that public dance halls were among "the most demoralizing social influences present in the modern city, directly or indirectly leading to the downfall of more girls than any other one agency." The Commission recommended that neighborhood social centers be established in churches, schools, or other buildings, as a means of improving the situation.

The founders of the Women's Welfare League responded to this call to combat the "bad moral influences surrounding young girlhood." They hoped to recruit other women from the women's clubs and churches of Minneapolis to assist in their fight against "moral laxness" and they hoped to "awaken among all women a strong protective sentiment toward the young women of the city."

While their first aim was to provide wholesome recreational facilities, the women of the League also wished to improve the living places of young women. Shortly after the Women's Welfare League was organized, an industrial census of the living conditions of Minneapolis working girls and women was made under the direction of Dr. Raymond Phelan of the University. The census found that there were over 19,000 working women in the city, and that Minneapolis ranked third in the United States in the number of homeless women. Supervised boarding homes in the city could take care of only a fraction of the women, and each of the homes had a waiting list. Of the 3,500 women the census-takers interviewed, twenty-two percent were living away from home.

One of the League's first projects was the Rest Home for Convalescent Women, opened in October, 1913, at 1801 Park Avenue. It was intended for "tired mothers" and employed girls and women who needed care during convalescence or who suffered from "overfatigue." The aims of the Home were listed as "health and character-building."

The Rest Home for Convalescent Women remained at this location until 1924, when it was moved to the old Loring Residence at Clifton and LaSalle Avenues. The Park Avenue house was then converted into the Club House for Girls, an emergency shelter for girls who had been referred by the Woman's Bureau of the Police Department and who would otherwise have been sent to jail. The Club House was for "young unfortunates," not "older, hardened repeaters who were considered workhouse cases." This residence served as the Club House for Girls until the late 1930s.

The Women's Welfare League was involved in various other ventures to help young women and to improve the moral environment of Minneapolis. The Linden Club, located at 1501 Linden Avenue North, was opened in September 1915 to serve as a safe and inexpensive home for working girls. Room and board at the Home ranged from $3.75 to $5.50 per week. The League also operated Fair Oaks, a home owned by the Minneapolis Park Board, as a city recreational and meeting center for young people working in business and industry. Meals were served to individuals or families and dances were given for young people. In 1920, community get-togethers were held at Fair Oaks on Friday nights, with a storytelling hour for children, a class in citizenship and current events for adults, and a musical program. Groups such as Campfire Girls and Girl Scouts met at Fair Oaks, and the Women's Welfare League encouraged use of the center as a meeting place for other civic and community organizations.

Presented with a petition signed by 350 young people that requested supervised dances to continue through the fall and winter, the League agreed to hold dances on the condition that those attending sign a pledge not to attend public dances.

The Cooperative Committee of the Women's Welfare League, incorporated in 1918 as the Women's Cooperative Alliance, had as its theme, "Arouse the community to its responsibility for prevention of juvenile delinquency." Participating in the Alliance were such organizations as the Council of Jewish Women, the Fifth District of the Minnesota Federated Women's Clubs, the League of Catholic Women, the Woman's Club, the Woman's Christian Association and the Woman's Christian Temperance Union; by 1920, there were 19 cooperating groups. The Women's Cooperative Alliance dealt with issues such as gambling, street carnivals, and regulation of child labor in the theaters, and, in 1920, the Alliance established a Citizens' Committee on Better Movies.

Other efforts of the League in the 1910s and 1920s included a resort lodge for working girls in Prescott, Wisconsin, a home for mentally deficient and delinquent girls, and nursing and boarding homes for elderly women. The League continued to operate a convalescent home at 100 Clifton Avenue until 1961.

SISTER KENNY INSTITUTE
27th Street and Chicago Avenue
Minneapolis, MN 55407

It was April, 1940, when Elizabeth Kenny (1880-1952), a self-trained Australian bush nurse, arrived in the United States to demonstrate her method of polio treatment. She went first to the Mayo Clinic in Rochester but was sent north to the Twin Cities because there were no polio patients at Mayo. In Minneapolis she found polio victims strapped into frames, splints, and casts—the crippling treatments she had fought for nearly thirty years.

Elizabeth Kenny had encountered her first case of polio in the Australian bush country near Brisbane in 1911. Little was known about the disease, so she did what seemed to her the "logical" thing for stiffened limbs: wrapped them in hot, damp cloths. She knew that muscle spasms were involved in polio and she could talk patients into moving muscles, sometimes within minutes. In some cases where doctors saw only paralysis, Kenny was able to discover a "live" muscle.

It was during World War I, when Elizabeth Kenny was serving as a war nurse for the Australian army, that she acquired the title "sister." She was promoted from "staff nurse" to the rank of "sister," which is equivalent to first lieutenant, in 1916 and retained the title for the rest of her life.

Minneapolis was the scene of Sister Kenny's greatest success. Minneapolis General Hospital established a clinic in 1941 to investigate her methods of treatment, and in 1942 the Hospital allowed her the use of the Lymanhurst building at 1800 Chicago Avenue for her work. The medical profession vigorously opposed her techniques, but the successful results at Sister Kenny's Minneapolis clinic eventually led to acceptance of her methods. Sister Kenny travelled throughout the United States and in Europe during the next decade to promote her method before returning to Australia in 1951.

The Elizabeth Kenny Institute at 1800 Chicago Avenue was dedicated in December 1942 to serve as a polio treatment center. When the discovery of the Salk and Sabine vaccines led to the virtual eradication of polio, the Institute expanded its services to treatment of patients with a variety of physical disabilities. In 1975 the Sister Kenny Institute merged with Abbott-Northwestern Hospital. Now located in the Sister Kenny Pavilion in the hospital complex, this comprehensive rehabilitation center is an impressive monument to Kenny's work.

DOMESTICITY
and the NUCLEAR FAMILY:
THE NEIGHBORHOODS of MINNEAPOLIS
TOUR

Linden Hills Boulevard, South Minneapolis, about 1924

REFER TO HEALTH CARE TOUR MAP PAGE 68

DOMESTICITY
Milwaukee Avenue
South Minneapolis
Around the Lakes

The settlement of Minneapolis and St. Paul took place at about the same time that new ideals of family life became dominant. The nature and character of both cities was conclusively marked by those ideals.

In the 1830s, the Anglo-American middle-class family began to show characteristics not common in the Western world in earlier times: marriage came to be based upon affection and mutual respect, and the wife came to have increasing influence. The woman in the marriage was seen to have, as her primary role, the care of children and home: this was her "sphere," as the Victorians commonly called it, and one of the symbols of its separateness and importance was the single-family home, within which the wife and mother held gentle dominion. With the force of her moral superiority (or so the ideals of the day would have it), she kept at bay and at a distance the increasingly ugly modern world.

Space, topography, and prosperity made it possible to realize the ideal of the single family home in Minneapolis and St. Paul on a scale seldom duplicated. Detached dwellings, no matter how small, were erected by generations of builders. Today, if you visit Milwaukee Avenue, not far from the West Bank Campus of the University of Minnesota, you will see that not only the rich could aspire to the privacy and independence the detached home provided. Milwaukee Avenue, its houses now restored to a condition of excellence and comfort they probably never had when they were new a century ago, was a street of workers' homes.

Much of South Minneapolis is made up of single-family homes of varying sizes and degrees of elegance. Driving south along Portland or Lyndale Avenues, one can pass through several miles of neighborhoods like these, none more than a few minutes from the downtown area. Along Minnehaha Parkway, the River Road, or around the lakes—Harriet, Calhoun, and Lake of the Isles—are more stately and ample dwellings. They are a mixture of architectural styles, most without particular distinction. Occasionally, especially in the neighborhood around Lake of the Isles, one will come across exceptions to this eclecticism. Purcell and Elmslie, two architects of the Prairie School which derived from Frank Lloyd Wright, designed a number of homes in the Twin Cities. What is particularly interesting about the Prairie School is that it represented a conscious effort to design homes that harmonized with the new ideals of family life. Its practitioners emphasized privacy, separation from the outside world, and interaction only among family members. Prairie School houses, though often sited on narrow urban lots, were positioned so that their inhabitants neither saw nor were seen by their neighbors. This ideal of privacy may be quite contrary to older notions of neighborliness and cooperation.

Domestic architecture, though seldom designed by women, suggests a great deal about the realities of women's lives and exercises a great effect upon them. The single-family home presumes a wife and mother to take care of it and make sure it fulfills the functions for which it was intended. It presumes that one wage-earner will be sufficient to meet the financial burden that such a home, wife, and children entail.

The realities of women's lives have changed greatly since the neighborhoods of Minneapolis were constructed. The Twin Cities, it is true, have been slower to feel the impact of those changes than have the cities of the east and west coasts: Minneapolis, for example, had no elementary school lunchrooms until very late in the 1960s. All children in kindergarten through sixth grade went home for lunch each day. The presumption was, of course, that their mothers were there.

Today, however, most married women work outside their homes, even when their children are very young. Financial necessity is the impetus in most cases, as it has always been. Inflation and high mortgage interest rates have become added imperatives in recent years. In the wake of a soaring divorce rate, the single-family home has become the single-parent home. In such situations, privacy and individualism are perhaps less valuable than cooperation and neighborliness would be.

As you tour these pleasant areas in the 1980s, you may speculate about what such changes mean for the women and the neighborhoods of the Twin Cities. Since the first elaboration of the domestic ideal, there have been some women who believed it held them hostage in the home. The first feminist movement, after all, arose in the nineteenth century, at the very time "woman's sphere" became defined and women's lives became, as the feminists thought, unfairly circumscribed. A century and a half later, in 1981, a study completed by General Mills revealed that most women would choose to be employed outside their homes, even if not compelled by economic need and even when they had young children. These women would prefer, however, to work part-time.

Such studies have provoked speculation about what this means for the workplace— how it will have to change in the future. Less attention has been given to what it means for the home of the future.

METHODOLOGY:

Researching Women's History

Researching to uncover the history of women in any town or city requires detective work. The first step is to try to imagine the major activities of women in the area: where they worked, where they lived, what churches they attended, and what cultural, recreational, and social welfare institutions they may have been involved in. State and local historical societies and libraries may have pictures, records of families and businesses and industries that employed women, biographical data about prominent citizens, and material on women's clubs and societies. Local history books may not have extensive information about women, but they often provide clues about where to look; the bibliographies, for example, may cite little-known books, pamphlets, or unpublished material about the area, and chronologies of local events often include references to the activities of women.

Another good place to begin research is *Women's History Sources* (R.R. Bowker, 1979), a guide to unpublished material on women throughout the United States. This monumental reference book is available at many libraries, historical societies, and archives.

Women played a vital role in founding and maintaining hospitals and social welfare institutions such as orphanages and homes for the aged. Annual reports, pamphlets and programs, minutes of meetings, and histories of such institutions are valuable sources of information. Women's organizations often have some sort of written history, if not more formal records such as minutes, correspondence, newspaper clippings, or account books. Researchers should contact local churches; many churches have published histories that contain sections about women's organizations. Church and synagogue records may also include minutes and account books of affiliated women's groups.

Old newspapers on file in historical societies, newspaper offices, libraries, or even in attics are a fruitful source of information: items on the women's page, notices of meetings of women's organizations, and articles concerning local events are often the only record of women's activities. Information can also be gleaned from old city directories and telephone books. In addition to the entries that begin with the words "women's" or "ladies'," there may be advertisements for women's businesses and enterprises. Finally, long-time residents of the area are sure to have ideas on who or what should be included in a tour and may be willing to share their knowledge of people and events.

The stories of women's lives contained in a tour such as this do not provide a comprehensive history of women in the Twin Cities. They do, however, increase our knowledge and understanding of the women who have lived here over the past century and a half. Driving along Summit Avenue, one is reminded of the tiring duties of immigrant domestic servants who worked in the mansions and lived in the upper floors. The hospitals of South Minneapolis bring to mind Martha Ripley and Sister Kenny, who challenged the medical establishment to offer innovative and effective health care to those with special needs. Passing by the North Star Woolen

Mill, one may think of the young women who labored in the garment mills and other factories in the late nineteenth and early twentieth centuries. It is hoped that these glimpses of women's lives and work in the Twin Cities will broaden our appreciation of the varied experiences of women and provide insight into the people and forces that shaped the development of this area.

Twin Cities native **KAREN MASON** has been involved in the study of local and women's history for several years. She worked with the St. Paul-Ramsey Bicentennial Commission, and, as a writer for the *Women's History Sources* project at the University of Minnesota in 1977 and 1978, Mason helped produce this major reference work which was published in 1979. A graduate of Bryn Mawr College in Pennsylvania, Mason received her Master's Degree in American history from the University of Minnesota, where her graduate work included research on women's organizations in early St. Paul. While attending the University, she was employed at the University's Social Welfare History Archives and at the Hennepin County Medical Center Archives. Karen Mason is now a doctoral student at the University of Michigan.

As a reporter for the *St. Paul Pioneer Press* and as a community faculty member at Metropolitan State University, **CAROL LACEY** has focused on the life and accomplishments of Minnesota women. She became associated with WHOM after writing about the organization's film project; her interest in the history of Minnesota women resulted in her MSU class, "Women in Minnesota." Among Lacey's independent writing, research and consulting work was participation in a nationwide, Carnegie-funded study of women in Campaign '76. Lacey holds a B.A. in music, English and German from Concordia College, Moorhead, an M.A. in journalism and political science, and a Ph.D. in American studies from the University of Minnesota. Her dissertation examined justice for children in twentieth century America.

DEBORAH CARLSON was president of Women Historians of the Midwest from 1978-1980 when the Women's History Tour was researched and written. She has taught English, history and special education in the Stillwater, Anoka and Minneapolis public schools. Carlson was graduated from St. Olaf College with majors in English, history and German; she holds M.A. degrees in education from The College of St. Thomas and in American studies from the University of Minnesota. She has done independent writing and editing in the areas of history and music. Her activities as a musician include performing chamber music in the metropolitan area, and serving as principal violist and current president of the Civic Orchestra of Minneapolis.

WOMEN HISTORIANS OF THE MIDWEST, an organization concerned with women in history, women in the historical profession, and non-traditional and alternative occupations for historians, was incorporated in 1973. Besides publishing a bimonthly newsletter which includes book reviews and articles, WHOM meets monthly from September to June, is a regional affiliate of the Coordinating Committee on Women in the Historical Profession, and a constituent member of the National Coordinating Committee for the Promotion of History.

Among WHOM projects have been three half-hour films on the history of women in Minnesota ("The Double Vision: Women in Education in Minnesota," "Homeward Bound: Women in the Family in Minnesota History," and "Collage: Minnesota Women in the Arts"), which were produced for educational television and are now available for sale or rental; the First and Second Conferences on the History of Women sponsored and organized by WHOM in 1975 and 1977; and several study groups, including a dissertation support group. WHOM also cooperated in the publishing of *Women of Minnesota, Selected Biographical Essays,* Stuhler and Kreuter

(Minnesota Historical Society Press, 1977). The Women's History Tour of the Twin Cities was researched and first presented in 1979 as an event at the American Studies Association Seventh Biennial Convention. The tour was given subsequently for local groups and organizations and was then developed as this book. In 1980 WHOM was the recipient of a major grant, from the Women's Educational Equity Act, to establish the Upper Midwest Women's History Center. The Center collects and catalogs women's history sources and materials appropriate for grades kindergarten-12. Summer workshops to train teachers to integrate women's history into their curricula, and women's history lessons, were produced by staff members of the Women's History Center during 1981. The Third Conference on the History of Women (April 30-May 2, 1982, at The College of St. Catherine) is the highlight of WHOM's tenth anniversary year.

SELECTED BIBLIOGRAPHY

Much of the information in the tour came from published and unpublished sources at: the Minnesota Historical Society's Library and Division of Archives and Manuscripts; the Minneapolis History Collection of the Minneapolis Public Library; the University Archives and Social Welfare History Archives, University of Minnesota; and the *Saint Paul Pioneer Press* Newspaper Library.

Published sources include:

Barsness, Diana. "Anna Ramsey: 'Shining Exemplar' of the True Woman," *Minnesota History,* Fall 1977, pp. 258-272.

Cohn, Victor. *The Woman Who Challenged the Doctors, Sister Kenny.* Minneapolis, University of Minnesota Press, 1975.

Foster, Mary Dillon, comp. *Who's Who Among Minnesota Women. A History of Woman's Work in Minnesota from Pioneer Days to Date, Told in Biographies, Memorials and Records of Organizations.* Privately published, 1924.

Holmquist, June D. and Jean A. Brookins. *Minnesota's Major Historic Sites: A Guide.* Saint Paul, Minnesota Historical Society, 1972.

Hurd, Ethel E. *Woman Suffrage in Minnesota: A Record of the Activities in Its Behalf Since 1847.* Minneapolis, Inland Press, 1916.

James, Edward T., ed.. *Notable American Women, 1607-1950.* Cambridge, Mass., The Belknap Press, 1971.

McClure, Ethel. *More Than a Roof: The Development of Minnesota Poor Farms and Homes for the Aged.* Saint Paul, Minnesota Historical Society, 1968.

Palmquist, Bonnie Beatson. "Women in *Minnesota History,* 1915-1976: An Annotated Bibliography of Articles Pertaining to Women," *Minnesota History,* Spring 1977, pp. 187-191.

Scovell, Bessie L. *A Brief History of the Minnesota Woman's Christian Temperance Union from Its Organization, September 6, 1877 to 1939.* Privately printed, 1939.

Sherman, John K. *Music and Maestros, The Story of the Minneapolis Symphony Orchestra.* Minneapolis, University of Minnesota Press, 1952.

Slack, Hiram Worcester, comp. *Directory of Charitable and Benevolent Organizations: A Classified and Descriptive Reference Book of the Charitable, Civic, Educational, and Religious Resources of Saint Paul, Minnesota, Together With Legal Suggestions.* Saint Paul, Amherst H. Wilder Charity, 1913.

Stuhler, Barbara, and Gretchen Kreuter, eds. *Women of Minnesota: Selected Biographical Essays.* Saint Paul, Minnesota Historical Society Press, 1977.

Weiner, Lynn. "Our Sisters' Keepers: The Minneapolis Woman's Christian Association and Housing for Working Women," *Minnesota History,* Spring 1979, pp. 189-200.

INDEX